Storytelling for Young Adults

Storytelling for Young Adults

A Guide to Tales for Teens

Second Edition

Gail de Vos

LIBRARIES
UNLIMITED
A Member of the Greenwood Publishing Group

Westport, Connecticut • London

British Library Cataloguing in Publication Data is available.

Library of Congress Catalog Card Number: 2003051648
ISBN: 1-56308-903-3

First published in 2003

Libraries Unlimited, Inc., 88 Post Road West, Westport, CT 06881
A Member of the Greenwood Publishing Group, Inc.
www.lu.com

Printed in the United States of America

The paper used in this book complies with the
Permanent Paper Standard issued by the National
Information Standards Organization (Z39.48-1984).

10 9 8 7 6 5 4 3 2 1

Copyright Acknowledgments

The author and publisher would like to thank the following for granting permission to reprint from their materials:

"Why All Tongues Are Red" by Dan Yashinsky. Copyright © Dan Yashinsky; to be published by Alfred A. Knopf Canada in *Suddenly They Heard Footsteps* by Dan Yashinsky. Reprinted by permission of Alfred A. Knopf Canada.

Excerpts from *Jasmine and Coconuts: South Indian Tales* by Cathy Spagnoli and Paramasivam Samanna. © 1999 Libraries Unlimited.

"The Phantom Ahead!" by Catherine Crowley.

"A Twist in Life" and "Taryn's Jump," by Taryn de Vos and Lawrence de Vos.

"Snake Back Ride" and "The King and His Jester," by Merle Harris.

"Old Frost and Young Frost," by Celia Barker Lottridge.

"The Twelve Months," in *Golden Axe* (Stotter Press, 1998) by Ruth Stotter.

"Gest and Maria," by Midori Snyder.

This book is for my daughter Esther, not only for her help and encouragement, but also for her irrepressible sense of humour and quest for justice.

Contents

Chapter 9: Sample Stories (*Cont.*)

Acknowledgments

The ultimate pleasure of being a storyteller is the friends you meet through sharing stories. I would like to thank fellow storytellers Catherine Crowley, Lawrence de Vos, Merle Harris, Celia Barker Lottridge, Cathy Spagnoli, Midori Snyder, Ruth Stotter, and Dan Yashinsky for their encouragement and for generously permitting me to include their stories in this volume.

Thanks also to the people at Libraries Unlimited, and particularly Barbara Ittner, for their patience and confidence. I would also like to thank them for publishing the World Folklore Series, an invaluable storytelling resource for storytellers for all audiences.

The greatest pleasure in writing this book has been the chance to collaborate with my daughter Taryn who did much of the initial finding of tales and helped write two of the stories. This has truly been a gift. Thank you.

Preface

When first writing about storytelling to young adult audiences, I was emphatic about the importance of listening to stories for this select age group. During the intervening years, I can only repeat myself, perhaps with even more emphasis (repetition being a time-honored aspect of the oral tradition), that storytelling should not be an option, but a necessity.

When *Storytelling for Young Adults* was first published more than a decade ago, I stated that there was a resurgence of interest in storytelling for all ages. This revival is still slowly gathering steam, but the perception of storytelling for young children is still in the forefront. Because storytelling continues to be regarded as mainly an activity for young children, not many young adults have had the pleasure or privilege of being told stories (or of telling stories). Convincing both young adults and the adults who work with them that listening to and telling stories should be an integral part of their lives is difficult for several reasons. First, young adults are very aware of their position in the transition from childhood to adulthood and do not want to be reminded of bedtime stories or library story hour. Second, adults who work with young adults often think of stories as something frivolous and lightweight, something that is a filler for when all the serious work and learning has been done.

This book is designed to again demonstrate to storytellers, librarians, educators, and parents the importance of telling stories to young adults. The first chapter echoes the pattern established by the first edition. It discusses the values of telling stories to young adults and the criteria for story selection. The focus of the second chapter is on telling stories to young adults, including nonverbal and verbal storytelling techniques as well as tips for telling scary stories. Much of what is included in this chapter also pertains to storytelling for all ages.

Chapters 3 through 8 provide a guide to appropriate tales for young adults that encompasses the world of literature from mythology to contemporary legends. *Storytelling for Young Adults* was written with the express purpose of helping storytellers and educators find good stories for the young adult audience. In the decade since its publication, a wealth of new material has been published for the telling, so the annotated stories in this volume have all been found in those books, the ones published in the 1990s and the early years of the new millennium.

The majority of *Storytelling for Young Adults* is organized by themes, each chapter containing annotations of stories. Included in each entry is the approximate time it takes to tell the story, a brief summary of the story, and the source, usually a collection of similar stories. Because the number of stories included in this volume is limited, they are only representative of the stories that appear in the collections referenced. These collections should therefore be searched for other good stories as well. I have included background information on the stories where I felt it was appropriate and when it was provided in the source notes by the author or collector of the tale. The final chapter includes twenty full-text tales that have been tried and tested with young adult audiences. These stories can be used as they appear, may easily be modified for your specific audience, or may be used as templates for building your own stories or for the young adult tellers themselves. Unless otherwise attributed, these retellings are mine.

The author, title, theme, and collections indexes will aid in locating appropriate tales.

Chapter 1

Storytelling and the Young Adult

> The greatest tales, well told, awaken the fears and longings of the listeners. Each man hears a different story. Each is touched by it according to his inner self. The words go to the ear, but the true messages travel straight to the spirit.
>
> —Juliet Marillier, *Son of the Shadows*

I have been storytelling to and with young adults for more than fifteen years now and continue to find that many adults and teenagers still assume that storytelling is something for children. I begin storytelling sessions by asking the members of the audience, "How many of you tell stories?" There is often laughter and some jeering, but I then ask them, " How many of you have ever made an excuse to a parent or teacher?" They look surprised and their hands shoot up high in the air. They start talking a bit louder as well. Now that I have their attention, I follow up with two more questions: "How many of you have ever told anyone about a book you have read, a movie you have watched, or a television program you have seen?" and "How many of you have ever passed along a juicy piece of gossip?" I then ask them the first question again, "How many of you tell stories?"

Once they realize that storytelling is something they do all the time, that storytelling is something we all do all the time, they are much more receptive to listening to tales.

> My experience as a storyteller and researcher suggests that teenagers are, contrary to popular opinion (including their own), very active and vibrant storytellers, using a rich repertoire of tales at a high level of competence as a means of social currency within their everyday conversational exchanges.. . . Teenagers tell personal experience narratives as much as anybody else, but it is the broad range of stories within their wider repertoires that is both surprising and significant, stories that display high levels of traditionality in their structures, motifs, and concerns. In fact, so much is this the case that I would say that teenagers are the unrecognized bearers and guardians of the same oral narrative traditions that can be glimpsed in the great folk and fairy tale collections. (Wilson 1997, 152)

Who Are Young Adults?

Eaglen (1983, 420) defines young adults as "that age group who no longer consider themselves children but are not yet considered adults by the adult world." Pedak (1978, 45) defines a young adult as "a member of the public who is in transition from childhood to adulthood; usually between the ages of thirteen to eighteen." In Canada and the United States, this encompasses people who are usually in junior high school and high school.

Adolescence is the term psychologists and educators use to identify the developmental stage marked by the onset of puberty and the end of structural physical growth. The term *young adult* is synonymous with *adolescent* and *teenager* but is preferred by librarians throughout the professional literature and so will be used in this book. For the purpose of this book, the term refers to people between the ages of thirteen and eighteen.

Telling Stories to Young Adults

> Every new generation of children belongs to the oral tradition, especially before they learn to read. The stories we tell them are their cultural and emotional history. (In Italian—as orally expressive a language as any—the word *sentire* means both "to hear" and "to feel.") Children want us to tell them where they came from, not where they're going, which, in any case, we have no way of knowing. The future they will forge for themselves, thank you very much. What we have to offer is the heroes and tricksters and helpers and witches and ogres who show them the way we've survived—or not survived—before. The future of storytelling is the past. (Hearne 2000)

But not only young children need these stories to aid them on their journey to maturity. The stories fulfill the special needs that young adults have as well.

These special needs include the need for entertainment and information, the need to belong, the need to learn in a social context, the need to experience responsibility, the need to establish a self-concept, and the need to communicate with adults who have an interest in them and their concerns (Amey 1985, 26). Storytelling, like reading books and watching films, is an activity that addresses these special needs by engaging the attention and the emotions of an audience. If the storyline works, the listener enters into the story and identifies with a character or situation portrayed. It is by entering into the story and "living" in it that young adults are open to the benefits of the experience. Listening to stories can serve as an outlet and testing ground for the strong emotions that young adults are experiencing and, in many instances, trying to camouflage. Conflicting values and roles can be explored through stories, because storytelling is a problem-solving activity. Characters in the stories are faced either with crisis situations or with common everyday concerns. Not only do members of the audience become aware of how others deal with problems similar to their own, but the stories also can be used to discuss alternate solutions to the problems.

I have been telling the story of "Mrs. Stone" for many years and in diverse environments. It is based on the writings of Mrs. Stone in her retrospective diary held in the special collections library at the University of Alberta where I teach storytelling. I was first drawn to her story, which you can read in Chapter 4, when I was researching historical tales for telling at Fort Edmonton Park, a historical museum where I was a resident storyteller for more than a decade "bringing history alive through story." I developed my telling from an episode that took place when Mrs. Stone was fifteen years old, after her father accidentally wounded her. Not only did this episode have high drama and demonstrate historical background, it was extremely relevant for the age of audience with which I usually worked. This story has had strong responses from diverse audience members, however. One elderly woman listened intently and then showed me her little finger (or, more correctly, the place where her little finger on her left hand should be). She then told me about a similar episode in her life and the consequences of losing her finger, particularly because she had dreamed of leaving the farm to become a secretary. "A secretary with no little finger on her left hand," she said scornfully. "But," she continued, "I decided I could become the best secretary there could ever be—and I did and I was!" This listener could identify with the historical period; it was not so distant from her own experiences. But what about young adults? At a storytelling session a few years later, a young man came up to me to say that he wished he had heard that story a few years earlier. He had lost his sight in one eye when he was fifteen but did not want it removed and replaced with a glass eye. The doctors insisted that it would be beneficial, and so, with the advice of his parents and his doctors, he did not resist. But, he told me, he had always regretted this decision. "If I would have heard this story before, I would have taken my courage from Mrs. Stone and fought for what I wanted."

Through story young adults are able to try out their own dreams, fantasies, fears, and concerns without experiencing real-life consequences. Storytelling keeps the young adult safe from consequences while strong, even extreme, emotions and roles are tried out in the stories. For this reason, storytelling has long been utilized as a tool for psychotherapy to mould a mentally stable individual (Yolen 2000).

> In one British secondary school for educationally subnormal children, weekly story hours are given . . . to selected second- and third-year pupils, aged thirteen–fifteen, who respond spectacularly to the fairy stories they never had in their disadvantaged childhood and to the stories and the excerpts which relate to their adolescent needs and interests in their contemporary surroundings. (Marshall 1975, 66)

Story hours should not be offered only to disadvantaged and learning-disabled young adults. All young adults can benefit from the therapeutic aspects of listening to stories. Konopka (1973) notes, in her key concepts of adolescence, that young adults have a need to experiment with their own strengths and value systems and must have an element of risk. Listening to stories offers the opportunity for experimentation in combination with safe risk taking.

The Values

In *Storytelling for Young Adults: Techniques and Treasury,* I isolated thirteen key reasons for young adults to listen to stories. I find that these reasons are still imperative, if not more so, ten years later as young adults rush down the information highway and are bombarded with innovative technology from all directions.

As an Aid in the Search for Identity

One of the major tasks confronting young adults is the development of a sense of personal identity. This search involves deciding what is important or worth doing and formulating standards of conduct for evaluating one's own behavior as well as the behavior of others. The expectations of peers and authority figures concerning the behavior and attitudes of young adults are aspects of this search for identity. Stories about people their own age, who are facing predicaments with which they can identify, help young adults in clarifying these expectations.

As mentioned previously, stories provide vicarious experiences for the listeners, and among these is the chance to probe various situations, roles, and values without suffering consequences. Storytelling offers the opportunity for experimentation. The needs of young adults to meet various kinds of people and from diverse cultures and to experiment with their own strengths and value systems can be answered in part by listening to appropriately selected stories that involve the listeners in contemplating themselves as individuals. Cultural stereotypes and archetypes abound in the body of folktales and fairy tales that are, in themselves, stories of the search for identity.

As an Aid in Developing Value Systems

Adolescence is the time when young adults examine the values, beliefs, attitudes, and ideas they have accepted uncritically and absorbed from their adult role models and accept, discard, and remold these values until they have established a value system that reflects the person who they are becoming. The challenge for young adults is to accumulate, organize, and evaluate enough values, beliefs, attitudes, and ideas to build their own system.

Besides opening a door to a world of values and beliefs, storytelling offers the insight that the search is universal. This is especially critical today, for not only are young adults in a state of flux, but the society with which they are trying to come to terms is also in a state of constant change. The search for a personal value system is related to the significant mental growth that is a factor in middle adolescence. This mental growth fosters an awareness of political and social systems previously unnoticed (Mitchell 1986). Young adults become conscious of the inconsistencies in society as they perceive the clash between the values exhibited by institutions and the general intent of the ideological system. Value confrontations are inevitable (Konopka 1973).

> Because of the conflicting values adolescents encounter in a rapidly changing world, they should have the opportunity to thrash out their reactions, consider the pluses and minuses, and try to determine where they themselves stand so that they will be better able to deal with ideas of all shades—including demagoguery. (Konopka 1973, 302)

Scharf (1978), in his review of Kohlberg's conventional level of moral judgment, stated that young adults during early adolescence have fixed definitions of social duty, concern with firm social rules, and a respect for formal authority. There is a shift in middle adolescence to a questioning of the moral order of the society. Rejection is a critical step for young adults in the process of defining themselves an autonomous value base. Storytelling offers, along with recognition of the universality of the search, insight into the motives and patterns of human behavior.

As an Aid in Establishing a Sense of Belonging

Young adults usually prefer to learn and to seek information within a social context. Storytelling brings young adults together for a shared purpose and reaffirms their sense of belonging to a group. Besides being included in a group, each member of the storytelling audience is included in the story as his or her needs for attention, security, belonging, or aesthetic satisfaction are met (Seaberg 1968). Konopka (1973), in her study of the conditions necessary for healthy development of youth, states that young adults need to have a sense of belonging both to their own age group and among adults. Storytelling can help fulfill this need because it can create a bond between the adult storyteller and the young adult audience.

As an Aid for Individual Contemplation

Listening to a story takes place in a group context, but every listener hears a different story and responds to it on the basis of his or her own beliefs, perceptions, ideas, experience, and needs. Eye contact between the storyteller and the audience helps to maintain the immediacy and intimacy of the sharing experience. Each member of the storytelling audience is sure that the story is just for him or her and that it pertains to the situation the individual is personally facing at that moment. Storytelling, as well as being a group activity, is intimate and respectfully private: listeners do not have to reveal to anyone their personal thoughts as they listen.

As an Aid to Encourage Emotional Release

Storytelling, along with reading and viewing films, encourages audience participation by offering an emotional release. By becoming involved in the storyline and the characters, young adults safely experience the emotions of the characters. The fear, anger, sorrow, lust, and laughter that the characters experience are experienced vicariously by members of the audience. Listening to the story engages the mind, supplants the everyday concerns of the listener, and frees members of the audience to experience—unselfconsciously—a rich and subtle range of emotions.

Young adults, who are constantly dealing with a multitude of emotional responses, struggle to maintain a "cool" façade. They wish to appear in total control over their emotions at all times. In many instances, this attempt at emotional control results in avoiding any display of emotional response. Young adults, listening intently to a story, unconsciously mirror their emotional responses on their faces as they interact with the characters, the storyline, or with a particular word choice they find appealing. The storytelling experience allows them a chance to relax their tight control.

I often suggest that teachers sit and watch their young adult charges from the front of the room when I am telling stories. There is no need to police them, I have not had any disturbances from young adults at any time while telling stories (the adults with them are sometimes a different story!). If you watch young adults' faces and body language, you see just how engaged they are with what they are hearing and vicariously experiencing.

As an Aid in Developing Imagination

One of the chief attractions of storytelling is that it is a participatory, rather than passive, activity. In television programs, movies, and video games, the concrete characters, the setting, and the action are all products of someone else's vision. While listening to a story, however, the audience has to imagine every scene, action, and character, all while listening intently to what the teller is saying and how said he or she is saying it. Television is a one-way means of communication, but in storytelling there is interaction between the teller and the audience; listeners are active participants, working with the teller to create images. The basis of creative imagination is the ability to visualize and fantasize. Storytelling informs, stimulates, and keeps alive the capacity to absorb and use information.

As an Aid in Entertaining

For any audience, listening to stories is relaxing and enjoyable. It is a time-honored form of entertainment and intimate sharing. "Since the stories are mirrors that reflect our passions and inclinations through the employment of archetypes and humor, we are entertained by laughing and crying over our own circumstances" (Livo and Rietz 1989, 11).

Young adults often react negatively to storytelling at the outset, thinking of it as an activity for young children; initially they can present quite a challenge to the storyteller. Some young adults have never heard a story told aloud and are reluctant to show any sign of interest or responsiveness (Barton 1986). It is not unusual for young adults to hover on the fringe of open-air storytelling sessions, at first to mock but eventually to listen. It is the enjoyment of the story—a story that is properly selected for the developmental age of the audience and told well—that converts the mockery of young adults to attentiveness and enjoyment.

As an Aid in the Creation of Bonds

An intrinsic part of storytelling is the direct and ever-deepening relationship between the teller and the listener (Simms 1983). The storyteller transmits not only the content of the story but also something of him- or herself, and individual members of the audience often reciprocate by sharing something of themselves with the teller. This bond between teller and young adult carries over into other activities that involve both of them—in the library, classroom, or home. Young people who were once members of a storytelling audience constantly approach me and say, "Do you remember me, you came to my school when I was in eighth grade?" I wish I could remember them all, but I certainly do remember some of their comments. Recently when shopping for graphic novels, one of the clerks said, "Ever since you told us stories, I have been afraid of spiders." When we started talking about the stories I told that day (the contemporary legend "The spider in the hairdo") , she said she was worried that I might be angry when she told me about it. "But," she continued, "I just had to say something when I saw you there." She had been in the eighth grade seven years earlier, but she still remembered the stories and the storyteller and felt a need to renew contact.

If librarians or teachers can create a climate of openness for the exploring young adult, they can play a vital role in the process of moral development (Scharf 1978). This ultimately leads to a satisfied clientele and to a developing adult community strongly supportive of public libraries and of education.

As an Aid in Developing Listening Skills

People in Western society, accustomed to a noisy existence, have conditioned themselves to ignore much of the noise around them, so much so that they no longer know how to listen. Less than half of the main ideas the average listener hears are retained (Briggs and Wagner 1979, 133).

Listening habits are primarily conditioned by the adult community. "A child now observes his adult models talking to each other as they watch their [television] programs and leaving him alone in the room during his program" (Briggs and Wagner 1979, 134). Briggs and Wagner feel that children no longer have adequate role models to aid in the development of listening skills. They made this comment about twenty-five years ago, and things have not progressed much since then. In fact, the popularity of computers and the Internet presents a new contribution to the problem. Today, in an attempt to keep down the chatter, movie theaters routinely warn theatergoers not to talk during the film by projecting a message on the screen. Such warnings now include reminders for people to turn off their cell phones. Unfortunately, such reminders cannot be broadcast in all public spaces. People are constantly chatting and not listening, regardless of their activity.

Egocentric young adults, as well as people from other age groups, tend to ponder their own thoughts and possible responses when listening to a conversation or lesson and do not fully attend to what the other person is saying. Communication skills are enhanced by listening to a variety of stories and tellers: young adults, their attention caught by a story, may develop the habit of listening courteously and critically. Well-developed listening skills are crucial to the education of young adults. Listening demands more of the audience than any other form of communication. In reading, it is possible to adapt one's rate to the difficulty or nature of the materials; difficult materials can be reread, unfamiliar words looked up, and there is time for reflection on one idea before proceeding to the next. These luxuries are not available for the listener, who must follow the speaker's rate regardless of the nature or content of what is being said. A listening audience must be able to recognize the meaning, intensity, color and inflection of the words the speaker uses to manipulate the audience.

Listening to stories is an extremely painless way to develop listening skills. Young adults should have the opportunity to hear many stories and many storytellers to develop the keen perception and alertness that is necessary to utilize their listening skills fully. Young children have short attention spans, and it is not until they are older that listening skills can be honed; unfortunately, as they grow up, listening to stories is no longer a common activity.

As an Aid in Preserving Traditions

Storytelling preserves traditional materials and methods of imparting information and knowledge. Not only does storytelling connect the present with the past by telling ancient tales in much the same way that they have been told for generations, but storytelling also offers young adults a world of traditions to aid them in their search for stability in an unstable time. The preservation and presentation of folk and oral traditions is a legitimate and valued service in and of itself.

As an Aid in Preserving Culture

In many cultures, storytelling has remained a powerful vehicle for the transmission of values, beliefs, and ideas. The stories of these cultures, because they provide essential channels for the communication of ideas, moral values, and observations on the behavior of the human species, have remained alive, meaningful, and relatively strong (Wolkstein 1974). Such stories are not commonly told in our society, even though they are available in print. Seldom do young readers actively seek out these resources, nor do they stumble upon them by chance. It is the storyteller who keeps our tales alive.

As an Aid in Developing Language Skills

Through the magical quality of the spoken word, storytelling reveals the charm and subtle connotations of word sounds and combinations, as well as the flow of rhythmic prose. Exposure to different tellers and storytelling styles allows young adults to recognize that language is personal. Oral language helps young adults to develop a descriptive style that they can use in expressing to others and to themselves the changes and emotions that they experience.

When listening to stories, young adults learn to appreciate and enjoy the sound of language. There is a strong fear, in this increasingly visual world of ours, that the diversity of word use will lessen. Jane Yolen, storyteller and young adult author, warns that people today face a serious deprivation: "the loss of the word, of words (Yolen 2000, 18).

Storytelling can help combat this danger, but to work well and to hold the attention of young adults accustomed to the visual stimulation of films, television, music videos, and video games, stories must be very strong.

As an Aid in Developing Discrimination

Storytelling can engender a love of story and lead young adults to books, but this goal, according to Sutton (1938), must be secondary. Sutton states that the primary reason for telling stories to young adults is to help them in their search for identity, values, and vicarious experiences. Briggs and Wagner (1979), on the other hand, feel that exposing young adults to literature that they may wish to read for themselves should be challenge enough for any storyteller. All storytellers agree, however, that listening to stories improves listeners' discrimination in their choice of books and stories for reading. Literary tales, told by a teller, introduce specific authors to an audience, and members of the audience frequently seek out either the same stories or additional material by the same authors because they enjoyed the telling.

This rationale, that storytelling leads to books, has kept storytelling alive in public libraries. The first library story hours were established for listeners over the age of nine because the children were expected to have mastered reading by that age (Greene and Shannon 1986). With the advent of widely published, high-quality picture books, librarians were quick to discover that using picture books in story hours was much more efficient than learning all the tales for the story hour. Consequently, "the more the story hour came to be associated with picture books, the more the older children stayed away, believing that such things were for 'babies' " (Pellowski 1977, 146). Today storytelling in libraries is directed almost exclusively at preschool and early-elementary schoolchildren. Rarely is telling stories to a group of young adults considered a library activity.

The Stories

Storytellers need to know where to find good stories before they begin the difficult task of preparation. They need more than a list of anthologies. They should know where to find stories for the interest level of the children. (Briggs and Wagner 1979, 47)

One of the pleasures of researching this book was the journey taken through the treasure trove of books and stories published in the last decade or so. The stories included in this volume are representative of the broadest array of cultures I could locate in widely available published sources. I also wanted to include diverse genres so that tellers and listeners with a wide range of interests could find relevant and enjoyable stories.

Criteria for Selection

I chose the stories included in this volume according to several criteria, as described in the following paragraphs. If more than one version of a story was available, I selected the version that best met the criteria.

Suitability

The story must be suitable for telling. I used the same seven characteristics of a good story used in *Storytelling for Young Adults,* characteristics originally put forth by Baker and Greene (1987, 29–30). According to Baker and Greene, a good story has the following features:

1. A single theme, clearly defined

2. A well-developed plot (A brief opening introduces the main characters, sets the scene, arouses pleasurable anticipation, and then, almost immediately, the story plunges into action. Action unfolds through word pictures, maintains suspense, and quickly builds to a climax. Each incident must be related in such a way that it creates a clear image in the listener's mind. The ending resolves the conflict, releases the tension, and leaves the listener feeling satisfied.)

3. Vivid word pictures, pleasing sounds, and rhythm

4. Characterization (The characters are believable, or, in the case of traditional folktales, they represent certain qualities, such as goodness, evil, or beauty.)

5. Faithfulness to the source material (Emaciated adaptation and vocabulary-controlled tales are not suitable.)

6. Dramatic appeal

7. Appropriateness for the listener

In addition, I only included stories that were published in English and that were not too difficult for the beginning storyteller to tell.

Availability

The source material had to be widely available. To be useful to storytellers, this bibliography includes only stories that have been published and can be easily located. For that same reason, I have not included stories that are published on the Internet because the content of Web sites, and the sites themselves, change without notice.

Recommendations

I selected stories from collections recommended by the literature or from stories familiar to me through storytelling experience. Practicing storytellers contributed many titles. Several of the full-text tales are not available in other print resources but are stories that I have developed and told. By putting them in print, I also confer permission to tell these stories but, as always, with proper accreditation of the source.

Appeal

The stories must appeal to a young adult audience. They must touch young adults, either by frightening them or by enlightening them about themselves or their own or other cultures. The stories must, above all, entertain.

Appropriateness for the Teller

A word of caution! Although these stories are appropriate for young adult audiences, they may not be appropriate for every teller. Each story must have meaning for the one who is telling it. If it does not, this will be immediately apparent to the audience, who may already view the procedure with skepticism. It is only through constant reading and experimentation with stories that tellers gradually learn to recognize what it suitable for them to tell. Please do not tell a story that you do not like. Pass it on to another teller so that the tale does not lose its power or freshness through indifferent telling. There are stories—perfectly good stories—that I am "allergic" to for one reason or another. Sometimes I understand the reasons behind my repugnance; other times, I only know that the story isn't for me. As you learn more about yourself as a storyteller, you will also learn more about yourself as a person. Learn to pay attention to your reactions to the tales when you first encounter them.

References

Amey, Larry. 1985. The Special Case for YA Programming. *Emergency Librarian* 12(3): 25–26.

Baker, Augusta, and Ellin Greene. 1987. *Storytelling: Art and Technique*. 2d ed. New York: R. R. Bowker.

Barton, Bob. 1986. *Tell Me Another*. Markham, ON: Pembroke.

Briggs, Nancy E., and Joseph A. Wagner. 1979. *Children's Literature through Storytelling and Drama*. 2d ed. Dubuque, IA: William C. Brown.

Eaglen, Audrey B. 1983. Services to Young Adults in Public Libraries. *Illinois Libraries* 65(7): 420–24.

Greene, Ellin, and George Shannon. 1986. *Storytelling: A Selected Annotated Bibliography*. New York: Garland.

Hearne, Betsy. 2000. Once There Was and Will Be: Storytelling the Future. *The Horn Book Magazine* (Nov.–Dec.): 712–19.

Konopka, Gisela. 1973. Requirements for Healthy Development of Adolescent Youth. *Adolescence* 8(31): 291–315.

Livo, Norma J., and Sandra A. Rietz. 1989. *Storytelling: Process and Practice*. Littleton, CO: Libraries Unlimited.

Marshall, Margaret R. 1975. *Libraries and Literature for Teenagers*. London: Andre Deutsch.

Mitchell, John J. 1986. *The Nature of Adolescence*. Calgary, AB: Detselig Enterprises.

Pedak, Maria. 1978. Public Library Programming for Young Adults: Frill or Necessity? *Drexel Library Quarterly* 14(1): 45–52.

Pellowski, Anne. 1977. *The World of Storytelling*. New York: R.R. Bowker.

Scharf, Peter. 1978. Moral Development and Literature for Adolescents. In *Young Adult Literature in the Seventies: A Selection of Readings*. Edited by Jean Varlejs. Metuchen, NJ: Scarecrow, 17–23.

Seaberg, Dorothy I. 1968. Can the Ancient Art of Storytelling Be Revived? *The Speech Teacher* 17(3): 246–49.

Simms, Laura. 1983. "Words in Our Hearts": The Experience of the Story." *The Horn Book* 59(3): 344–49.

Sutton, Roger. 1983. Telling Tales for YAs. *School Library Journal* 30(3): 44.

Wilson, Michael. 1997. Teenage Tales. *Children's Literature in Education* 28(3): 151–62.

Wolkstein, Diane. 1974. An Interview with Harold Courlander. *School Library Journal* 20(9): 19–22.

Yolen, Jane. 2000. *Touch Magic: Fantasy, Faerie and Folklore in the Literature of Childhood*. Expanded ed. Little Rock, AR: August House.

Chapter 2

Telling the Tales

> When the body of a story is stretched out before us,
> we who are new to the telling of tales sometimes
> don't know where to make the first cut. Which is
> the best way to enter? Shall we plunge deep into the heart
> of the matter or begin systematically with the extremities?
>
> —Sheri Holman, *The Dress Lodger*

It is unfortunate that the term *storytelling* carries a negative connotation for the average young adult. Although the teacher or librarian can easily introduce a story into a regular classroom activity without any label, any storytelling activity that is based on voluntary attendance must be carefully named if it is to attract an audience of young adults. A program titled "Horrible but True: Happenings in the Neighborhood" will appeal more strongly than one titled "Urban Belief Legends" (unless the audience members think they will be viewing the two movies that carry a similar title). The term *storytelling* need not appear in the title of the program or the description that accompanies it.

What Is Story?

A story is a structure that encompasses a beginning, a middle, and an end and is the most effective tool we humans have for making sense of our world and ourselves. Of all oral stories, the ones with the greatest power are the ones that come from within: our own stories. To be worth listening to, however, these personal experience stories must be formed and polished with the same care and attention we give to more traditional tales. Traditional folklore is also charged with great authority. These tales have been polished and repolished over the years to teach lessons, to remind us of our similarities and differences, and to offer both validity for our beliefs and values as well as goals and direction in times of stress and fear. Because so much of our literature and popular culture is based on traditional folklore, motifs, and archetypes, it is essential that we are familiar with these stories.

Introducing the Concept of Storytelling

Before telling stories to a group of young adults for the first time, in either a school or a public library setting, introduce the concept and practice of telling stories. Depending on the situation, this may be done in brief or in a more comprehensive manner. When I am a guest teller in a school, I always begin the session by asking the students if they tell stories. I then tell them that the stories I tell are the same as theirs, only that I take them home and polish them before telling them to an audience. Before telling any other stories, I then introduce myself, my background, and my books through a personal experience story. I use this story as a gauge to see what type of listening audience I have; if they laugh when I expect them to, I can tell them certain types of tales and so on. I start this way:

> I never wanted to be a storyteller when I was growing up. In fact, I had never even known there was such a profession. I grew up in a small town in the middle of Alberta. The entire time I lived there I had one goal—to leave! I knew that my real parents were not my real parents. My REAL parents were very wealthy, and I knew that if I could just find them, they would give me a lot of money and I would never have to work. So my game plan was simple—graduate from grade twelve, move to Edmonton (the closest city), get a passport, and go looking for those very rich parents.
>
> And that is exactly what I did. I graduated from grade twelve, moved to the University of Alberta where I spent four years to become a junior high school teacher, a history teacher. When I graduated from the university, I got the government of Canada passport and went traveling. I spent one year, teaching Australian history in Australia, and then I moved on to South East Asia, to Laos, where I taught English as a second language. I was there when the Pathlet Lao took over the country, ending a civil war

that had been fought for more than forty years. When they did that, they kicked out all Western people. This time I didn't want to leave, but I had no choice. So I came back to Canada with one idea in mind—to earn enough money to go traveling. By this time I had learned two important things about myself. One, I loved to travel. Two, my real parents were my REAL parents, and they didn't have a lot of money. So if I wanted to have some, I had to earn it myself.

I got a job selling stereos and records. It was the same job that had put me through university, and I had just about saved enough money when one Thursday night, this blond guy came into the store. He had bought a record the day before and it had a scratch on it, so he had come to complain a little and exchange it. I took one look at him and thought, "Not bad!" So I asked him if he wanted to talk about it over coffee.

I am still not sure that was a bright move—I didn't go traveling, I got married, and we have two daughters. When the girls were young, I decided to go back to school and become a librarian. Because I wanted the girls to get used to their mom being a student, I decided to take a night course. The first night course at the library school was storytelling. I never wanted to tell stories; I was terrified of large groups. I have problems speaking English, and it is the only language I know. But I looked at my daughters and thought, "I can practice on them." So I took the course and I got caught. I got caught by the power of story and the power of storytelling. I finished my degree. I am a librarian. But I have never worked in a library; I became a storyteller.

I continue on my tale, introducing the books and courses I teach before I tell any of the other stories. I have created bonds between the audience and myself by opening myself up to them and establishing a comfort zone. They become familiar with my speech patterns, my storytelling style, and my love for story without realizing it.

Choosing the Right Story

After you have attracted the interest of the young adult audience, it is essential to keep that interest. The first story that you tell to young adults is of the utmost importance: it is the hook that captures your audience. It is imperative that you, the teller, really like the story and know it well. The teller must also be comfortable with the audience and the storytelling situation. I recommend starting with a ghost story or an urban legend, but if you have problems telling these kinds of tales, as some people do, begin with a strong, evocative myth.

I cannot emphasize enough the importance of selecting a story that is appropriate for both the audience and the teller. This book contains approximately two hundred suggested stories that are appropriate for young adult audiences, but not all of them are appropriate for every storyteller. The teller must enjoy the story to tell it successfully. If you are unsure of or unhappy about any aspect of the story you tell, the audience will also be unsure and unhappy without knowing why.

The best place to locate a story for the telling is in the world of folklore. Folklore is the umbrella term that encompasses folktales and fairy tales, myths, legends, nursery rhymes, contemporary legends, ballads, epics, and other story material that has no identifiable author. This material belongs to the public domain and is waiting for you to discover it, shape it, and make it your own. This is one of the reasons there are so many annotations from the world of folklore in this volume. A second reason is that these stories have been polished and shaped throughout time, and only the best, the most relevant, and often the most appropriate have been passed down through the ages and set in print.

Before you learn a story, you should research it. To do the story justice, the teller must know something about the origin of the story; the background and motives of the author if it is a literary tale, and the culture and characters that are introduced in the story. Read as many versions or adaptations of the story as you can find. This will help you formulate your own perception of the characters, action, and resolution. It is this perception that you will transmit to the audience in your version of the story. I usually recommend finding at least three versions of a story you want to tell and reading them carefully. Then, put the texts away and tell the tale in your own words. You will subconsciously amalgamate the versions into one that is unique to your own understanding of the tale. One responsibility of storytellers is to adapt stories to make them more relevant to today's audiences, but storytellers also have a responsibility to the story itself.

> Modifications and modern adaptations are generally acceptable if, warns Laura Simms, the changes "protect the intrinsic value of the story." But most storytellers agree that some stories should *never* be changed: sacred, ritual stories in reverence for the culture and its tradition, and literary tales out of respect for the author's literary process, labor and love. (Smith 1988, 322)

In my university courses on storytelling, the students must research the folktales they have selected to tell for their final assignment. I introduce them to Margaret Read MacDonald's (1982) *The Storyteller's Sourcebook* to help them find motifs and variants of the stories they have selected. We also discuss the two articles by Betsy Hearne (1993) on citing and respecting the source. These articles focus on authority and source notes in picture book versions of folktales, but I have expanded it in my classroom to include all collections of folktales.

Most of us who have been storytellers in modern times know that it is common courtesy to acknowledge sources, whether we've heard the story from someone else or read it somewhere. More than manners, this practice also sets the story into a framework that is *part* of the story, giving listeners a context for the story world. Oral cultures provided this context naturally; most stories were told in traditional settings, either domestic or ritualistic. If stories were introduced cross-culturally, they came a few at a time and were absorbed over time. Adaptation was a long-term process, and stories were a community heritage well known to listeners. Their expectations of a story were primed by context, and their understanding was shaped by that context. (Hearne 1993, 22)

Students must also provide a story structure or map for their stories. Although I do not require a specific type of story mapping, I do model several methods for them. By reducing their story to a story structure, they discover which elements in their stories are important while reducing the tendency to memorize the story verbatim. Storytelling is not memorization; it is the active unveiling of a tale before the audience, an unveiling that involves both the teller and the audience as they enter the world of the story between them and create it anew each time. This can only be accomplished if the teller is completely at home with the story—if he or she understands the plot, setting, and characters and can experience it with all five senses. We explore setting and the characters in the stories, focusing on the character traits and motivations of the characters rather than physical attributes. My stories and the stories my students learn are character-driven rather than plot-driven stories. This gives the tales their power, their immediacy, and their relevance. Everything should be for the service of the story, for it is the story that is of utmost importance. Respect the story, the culture from which it derives, and the previous tellers who have helped shape the tale. This does not mean that the tellers cannot make the story their own; they must do so. But when you understand the story and the culture and era from which it has sprung, the spirit of the story lives on.

How to Tell Stories

Storytelling to young adults involves eradicating the barrier of program labels that carry negative connotations, choosing stories that appeal to both the audience and the teller, telling the story well, and having little expectation of audience response. It is a challenge to face this age group and tell a story, but telling stories to young adults is not so different from telling stories to other age groups. In all situations, tell the story in a sincere, straightforward manner, in your natural voice. Young adults appreciate being spoken to as if they were your peers and will definitely tune you out if they feel you are condescending in any way. Sound effects may be added to your telling, but only if you do them effectively and use them sparingly. Nothing distracts an audience as much as a poorly executed bark or the constant repetition of the same sounds. This technique in storytelling may be effective with preschoolers but will quickly lose a young adult audience. Do not be afraid of silence and pauses within your story. Pauses are effective tools in the telling of stories and are necessary to enable the audience to see and experience the action, setting, and characters of the story while it is being told.

The Five Languages of Oral Storytelling

Storyteller Donald Davis (1993) talks about the five languages of oral storytelling in *Telling Your Own Stories*: gesture, sound, attitude, feedback, and the words themselves. I refer to them continuously when teaching storytelling because they are, indeed, essential elements of the art of telling a tale.

Gestures

Gestures, those limited physical movements that enhance the communication process, are the most natural language that we possess. All of us use body language (and not just hands and faces) to engage a listener in conversation. How often do we use gesture instead of words? For beginning storytellers, however, this language is often a difficult one to incorporate and become comfortable using. Gesture, which is the suggestion of action rather than the acting out of an action itself, lends itself well to the blossoming of the listeners' imaginations but should be used sparingly, because it can easily distract an audience that has been raised on visual images. Instead of focusing on and listening to the words of your story, the audience will follow your gestures. When employing gestures, make sure that they grow out of the context of the story, that they either proceed or accompany the words spoken, and that they are natural for you. Poorly placed or awkward gestures will result in audience members being propelled out of the story world, and they may resist entering that world again. It is important to realize that not all gestures are universal and that they are culture-specific. If you are telling stories to an audience outside of your regular cultural base, it is advisable to research the nonverbal language of that culture before telling your stories.

Sound

Davis (1993) explains this language as the way words actually sound. The word on a page may have a different sound for different readers, and it is up to the individual storyteller to decide how that word is articulated. This colors the interpretation of the story, the characters, and the sympathy of the audience. (Say "mother" as my young adult daughters usually sound it! Or say it softly as if you saw your dear elderly mother fast asleep on the couch—or perhaps not so softly after all.)

Attitude

Attitude is an important language and one that is often overlooked when talking about telling stories. It is the attitude of the storyteller him- or herself: how the storyteller feels about the story, the characters, the audience, the situation, the time of day. All of these factors affect the way the story is told. I try to instill in my students that they should look at a well-prepared story as a gift that the storyteller has selected, wrapped, and presented to the audience. If the storyteller is sincerely pleased to be giving that gift, the story will flow and accomplish all that the teller wishes it to, as long as the teller has prepared the tale well. The teller must be comfortable with the story and the situation. Any discomfort on the part of the teller will be immediately transferred to the audience.

Feedback

Feedback, in this instance, refers to the immediate response to the story as it is being told. Because storytelling is a temporal art form, it cannot exist without an audience—and if you are blessed with a receptive audience, the story will burst forth almost spontaneously. If the audience seems to be responding negatively, it is often hard work making your story live. This aspect of storytelling is an essential one for people working with young adult audiences. The teller must be comfortable with the story, so much so that she or he can be concentrating on those miniscule examples of positive feedback from the typical young adult audience. Tellers who are expecting an overt reaction from the audience often blame themselves when they do not receive it from the young adults. In most cases, it is not a negative response but simply a matter of the teller not recognizing the reaction and feedback that can be expected from a given audience. When telling to young adults, expect a minimum of overt feedback. If they are listening respectfully and quietly, that should be a strong enough message that what the teller is doing is appreciated.

Words

Because the words on the page are often the starting point for storytellers, beginning tellers want to memorize these words and pay little attention to adding the other four languages to the mix. For the stories to live, the teller needs to incorporate his or her own words (not those on the page) with gestures that are appropriate to the teller and the story and with sounds that reflect the teller's own interpretation of the characters and plot. There should be a chance for the story to be told to various audiences during the learning process so that the teller can learn and adapt the tale from audience feedback. The storyteller should also be enjoying the process throughout the finding, learning, polishing, and telling of the story.

Storytelling Techniques

What is it that makes one told story and one storyteller more memorable than another tale or teller? It usually can be attributed to the way in which the teller incorporates basic storytelling techniques such as eye contact, understanding audience expectations, timing, natural confidence, and being true to oneself and the story.

Eye Contact

Eye contact is one of the most important storytelling techniques. This may prove to be one of the most daunting aspects of telling stories to young adults. Members of this audience, unless they have recently been exposed to the pleasures of listening to stories, adopt a bored, glazed look that retains a trace of cynicism. At the beginning of the session, they are conscious of the reactions of other members of the audience and do not want to react any differently from their neighbors. They may return your eye contact with stares or challenges. Proceed with enthusiasm and confidence, and tell your story well. The listeners will quickly realize that you enjoy the story and are telling it so they can enjoy it as well.

Expect Little Response

The most important thing to remember when telling stories to young adults is not to expect any overt response. A young adult audience may not demonstrate any appreciation or evidence of listening to a story. Do not assume, however, that the story has not had an effect. Young adults are hesitant to display their feelings, particularly in a large group. Time must be allowed for individual members of the audience to absorb the story and to relate it to their own experiences and background.

Of course, there are always pleasant surprises. When telling urban legends, which I usually do in a workshop-type setting, telling the tales and giving some background on them and why they are being told, most young adult audiences become animated and ask questions throughout my presentation. Rarely do I finish one of these sessions without one or two members of the audience coming up to me to tell me their versions of the stories.

One of your biggest barriers may be the negative expectations of the teachers and administrators to a storytelling session. I remember coming into a high school where the librarian who had hired me had moved on and just left instructions that I was coming to tell stories to the high school students. The principal met me at the door and explained that he and the teachers had everything under control. Although they were not sure what I would be doing, they had arranged for the students to be seated in the gym—my absolute least favorite place to tell stories. While gymnasiums are perfectly fine for sporting events, their very construction works against the intimacy necessary for successful storytelling. There is always an echo present, even though the voice immediately soars into the rafters and away from the ears of the audience.

The principal had all the teachers standing around the perimeter of the gym to make sure that they could immediately pull out any misbehaving student. "Not too worry," he reassured me. Not to worry? I was appalled and apprehensive about overcoming the barriers the teachers had set up for me before I even walked into the gym. As I entered the room, a student sitting in the front row jumped up and squealed, "It's her!" She turned to the audience and in a loud carrying voice said, "Hey, you guys, listen up. Remember that storyteller I told you about that I heard when I was in junior high? This is her—and she is going to tell you the same stories!" She sat down and beamed at me after reminding me what stories I had originally told her. I threw away the program I was planning on telling and told the same stories I had before. The teachers did not have to police their students, and I got rave reviews. Actually, I have never had problems controlling any of the young adult audiences to which I have spoken and told stories. I simply tell them good stories and respect them without expecting too much in return.

The Art of the Pause

The pause is the silence between words, phrases, scenes, or sentences that allows the audience time to reflect, react, or anticipate what is happening in the story or what will happen next. It should not be confused with hesitations. Too often, beginning storytellers are afraid of the pause—afraid that their audience may think that the storyteller has forgotten what comes next or afraid of the silence itself. We do have a tendency to be afraid of silence, so we have space fillers to compensate for them: "umn," "and so," "like," and others rush in to fill the spaces that a thoughtful pause creates.

Effectively used, pauses help us achieve clarity, emphasis, and emotional quality for the audience. They also provide the storyteller with a natural opportunity to take a breath. Following are a few ways to use pauses.

- Pause before you start your story. After you arrive in front of your audience, center yourself, pause, breathe, and smile while you check to make sure that the images for your opening to the story are there and ready to use. Do not start your story until the audience is ready to listen. Because I like to get as close to my audience as possible when telling stories, when in the classroom, I walk in front of my desk to tell stories. This is a signal for the class, but it also gives me a chance to get in touch with the story I am planning on telling.

- Pause regularly. Pause and make sure the images of the next scene are ready to be told. Using pauses becomes more natural when you think in images or scenes rather than in words. When thinking in images, we tend not to concentrate on the words, rushing through them on the way to the end of a story, but to focus on the most effective way of helping the audience experience the images you are unfolding with them in your telling.

- Because we often rush stories, particularly when we are nervous, adding pauses is good for both the audience and the teller. Allow the audience time within your story to breathe and to contemplate. Remember, also, to provide them with rushes of activity and excitement in keeping with the action of the story. When a storyteller pauses after a pause, the audience eagerly awaits the next part of the tale; their interest is heightened and their comprehension increased.

- Include a variety of pauses. Solemn, profound, and complex material generally demands longer pauses than lighter, simple, or familiar tales. There are exceptions to this, of course. Punch lines or laugh words can often be made funnier if preceded with a relatively long pause. The art of telling a ghost story depends on the effective use of a variety of pauses.

- Pause when you are finished. Don't move when you have finished your story. Stay standing (or sitting) where you are, and breathe, smile, and acknowledge the adulation of the crowd before moving away. Of course, if you are telling to young adults, you have to judge just how long you should pause here, because it is sometimes difficult to perceive any adulation!

- Play with the pause and your sense of timing when practicing your story. You will soon realize where to place the pauses and how long to make them to build suspense and drama and to develop your characters. Have fun with silence!

Listening is hard work. Allow breathing space between the telling of one story and the next or follow-up activity. The breathing space can take the form of a brief introduction to the next story or information about the story just told. During this pause, you may explain why you are telling the story or give some background on the culture that produced the story or on the author who created it.

In the last few years, I have been incorporating several string stories into my young adult programs as a break between tales. String figures are structures created from a loop of string with the hands, usually by one person, but sometimes two, as in the well-known string game, "Cat's Cradle." They are probably the most widespread of all games, being found in nearly all cultures. Stories told in conjunction with the making of a string figure are also common to almost all cultures. I had used string stories without qualification with younger audiences but shied away from using them with young adults. I tell stories at the local folk festival in Edmonton, and when I was first asked to do it, the organizers assumed that the storytelling audience would be young children. They soon discovered, however, that large numbers of young adults gathered to watch my string stories. The young adults would patiently wait while we told stories to young children and then would come back and ask me to teach them how to do the string figures. With their interest in mind, I told a string story, along with the story of how I learned string stories, to a high school audience. It was an unqualified success, and I have included at least one or two string tales in my programs ever since.

Prevent Distractions

A brief opening to each tale should point out any aspects of the story that may distract the audience. Do not assume that high school students understand seldom-used words or allusions to specific cultures. A colleague of mine told an Inuit myth to a eleventh-grade Canadian class, assuming that the students were familiar with both the vocabulary and the Inuit culture. In the opening minutes of the story, she used a term several members of the audience did not understand. In horror, I watched the ripple created by as audience members nudged their neighbors to ask if they knew what the word meant. By the time the story ended, the concentration of more than half of the listeners had been disturbed, leaving the teller shaken and the tale virtually unheard. Beth Horner suggests the following: "Before some myths I point out that some parts of a story (such as falling in love with the moon) may seem 'stupid' and 'unrealistic.' I suggest that if they simply accept these 'unrealistic' elements as part of the story and not let them be distracting, they will enjoy the story more" (Horner 1983, 461). This eliminates the need for members of the audience to react negatively at that point in the story in order to demonstrate to their peers that they are too mature to be taken in by such nonsense. If everyone already knows it is nonsense, there is no need for such demonstration. The audience will instead listen and experience the tale as it is told.

Appreciate the Story as Story

There is a tendency in the school environment to follow each enterprise with a meaningful activity. Although there are countless ways of integrating story into the curriculum at all levels and in all subjects, it is imperative to remember that it is not necessary to analyze a story after telling it, and, in fact, most storytellers highly discourage it. Analysis can be insulting to the teen listener and can kill interest in the story (Horner 1983).

Telling Scary Stories

Almost everyone likes a good ghost story or scaring another person with a well-told tale. There is no one "correct" formula for telling this type of tale, for each teller must determine and depend on his or her own strengths as a teller. Kathryn Windham suggests that the storyteller simply be natural and let the tale stand on its own. "Excess drama or affectation simply takes away from the magic of the story. The audience must hear the story, not see the teller. Above all, don't try to explain the story to the audience" (Unverzagt 1999, 6).

It is not the storyteller's role, however, to analyze those fears that lurk in the unconscious of each listener, but to offer an opportunity in a safe setting for listeners to confront and master these fears indirectly without having to even admit that such fears exist. To accomplish this requires that the teller know the audience well (an essential ingredient *any* time), understand [its] levels of development (individually and as a culture), and be sensitive to [its] belief systems, regardless of how valid or invalid those beliefs may seem. (Kevin 1999, 23)

Know Your Audience

I must offer a caveat here because tellers of scary tales are also the ones who are frequently targeted by people who are uncomfortable with the topic of the supernatural. Please be aware of the audience and of the religious beliefs of the majority, if at all possible. You must respect their beliefs and refrain from telling tales that will offend. The important word in this suggestion is "majority." All too often, it is the one or two outspoken individuals who are heard. This is a judgment call for storytellers. Likewise, I am uncomfortable telling scary stories to younger audiences and therefore will not do so. This is a reflection on myself as a mother; my daughter's nightmares were evidence enough for me that she was too young for this type of story. By the time students are in sixth grade, however, they should have the maturity to handle this type of tale.

Promote Ambiguity

In their tips for telling scary stories, the editors of *Storytelling World* suggest the following:

> Terror is more convincing when suggested or evoked than when explicitly documented. Go for suggestion over definition. Apparitions, for example, may seem all the more ghostly if they remain vague and ill-defined, as hazy in the listener's mind as they are in the story character's vision. People love mysteries, and despite attempts by some to pry out the answers, most listeners will relish a story longer if it leaves some issues unresolved, something for them to think about and discuss later. (Kevin 1999, 14)

Genuine Emotions

The most successfully told scary stories are experienced by both the teller and the audience at the same time. The teller of these tales, as with all tales, should evoke all senses of the listener to make the story come alive. "Apprehension is enhanced when suggestions of terror come through ominous sounds, a chilling touch, strange fetid odors, or a repulsive taste, as well as through the typical visual clues" (Kevin 1999, 14). At the same time, tellers must portray the feeling themselves in the use of voice, gestures, facial expressions, and physical stance. "Avoid *describing* feelings. Help your listeners actually *experience* the emotions of the story characters. It's what they long for in 'scary' stories" (Kevin 1999, 14).

Suspense and Secrets

Timing is essential for a well-told scary story. Build up slowly to the climax, prolonging the suspense and leaving the conclusion climatic and mysterious. Do not explain it away. "Attempts at natural explanation are a form of cheating, a salve for the teller's conscience and detrimental to the scary experience for the audience" (Kevin 1999, 14). Often, when doing a workshop or school presentation on contemporary legends, I tell the story and then explain why I used certain elements in it. This is not to explain away the mystery, but to demonstrate that the tales need plausibility, and often research, to work effectively. I am providing background into the storyteller's craft and, at times, the history of the story, but I always leave listeners to interpret the story on their own.

Teen Tellers

> [The storyteller] must not simply be a mouthpiece for artistic excellence, but must seek to encourage students to bring their own stories to the session, to make the classroom a safe place to tell stories, an environment where they will be valued and appreciated as the works of literature and skilled performance they undoubtedly are.. . . If we genuinely value the students' own culture, we may be able to develop a more effective expression of that culture alongside a wider appreciation of different kinds of oral literature and performance, and so become a gateway to other areas of English and Drama work. If we are really going to capture the imaginations of teenagers with storytelling, then we need to give them credit for the performance and literary skills that they already have and attempt to enhance them. (Wilson 1997, 156)

Although there are many ways of learning a story, there are really no age-related differences that I can isolate for teens in learning a tale. The most vital aspect of learning a story to tell is that the story be one that the teller likes a lot. It must also be appropriate for the intended audience and environment. These two criteria must be kept foremost in mind when encouraging teens to tell their tales.

When encouraging teens to tell stories, their teachers often focus their energies on telling tales to younger audiences. Although this is a laudable exercise, I highly recommend encouraging teens to tell to their peers. This should help them overcome any fears of speaking in front of their own age group. This is one of the largest obstacles some of my university students must overcome to tell their tales. Telling to a young audience is not a threat, but telling to their classmates seems to be.

References

Davis, Donald. 1993. *Telling Your Own Tales*. Little Rock, AR: August House.

Hearne, Betsy. 1993. Cite the Source: Reducing Cultural Chaos in Picture Books, Part One. *School Library Journal* 39(7): 22–27.

Hearne, Betsy. 1993. Cite the Source: Reducing Cultural Chaos in Picture Books, Part Two. *School Library Journal* 39(8): 33–37.

Horner, Beth. 1983. To Tell or Not to Tell: Storytelling for Young Adults. *Illinois Libraries* 65(4): 458–64.

Kevin, Jim. 1999. Scary Stories: Information for Tellers. *Storytelling World* 16 (summer/fall): 13–25.

MacDonald, Margaret Read. 1982. *The Storyteller's Sourcebook: A Subject, Title, and Motif Index to Folklore Collections for Children.* Detroit, MI: Gale.

Smith, Jimmy Neil, ed. 1988. *Homespun: Tales from America's Favorite Storytellers.* New York: Crown.

Unverzagt, Kathy. 1999. Kathryn Windham: The "Ghost Lady." An Interview. *Storytelling World* 16 (summer/fall): 4–6.

Wilson, Michael. 1997. Teenage Tales. *Children's Literature in Education* 28(3): 151–62.

Chapter 3

Tales of the Fantastic

*B*ut given what human beings have done, practiced and believed in the last ten thousand years, it's quite hard to make up anything new and it's a shame to see the old stuff lost, since I doubt that a great deal of it is now electronic. If the signposts I can give get a few people reading real books, and getting a feel for the *depth* of their society, then I think I'll have done my job.

—Terry Pratchett, "Imaginary Worlds, Real Stories: The Eighteenth Katherine Briggs Memorial Lecture"

Fantastic is a term that has been adapted as a general term for all forms of human expression that are not realistic, including fantasy, science fiction, magical realism, and so on. In this case, fantastic refers to tales that horrify, scarify, and twist perceptions of reality. Stories that evoke these emotional and mental states are all extremely popular with young adults. Scary stories can serve the same role that traditional folktales once played: they give the listeners an opportunity to experience their deepest fears vicariously in their subconscious and to stretch their imaginations. Thus, the young adult audience does not need to confront directly what they may not yet be prepared to face (Kevin 1999, 15).

31

Courage in the face of danger is a highly valued trait in any culture: the warrior who stands alone against superior numbers of the enemy; the mother who confronts fire or flood to save her children; the virtuous youth who elects death over dishonor. But courage is not the *absence* of fear; it is a learned ability to *master* one's fears and to carry on nobly in the face of danger. Fear enhances survival. If terror propelled our ancestors away from predators, they lived long enough to produce another generation. If diseased flesh and decaying corpses filled them with horror and revulsion, they avoided those sources of infectious or contagious diseases, thereby extending their life spans. (Kevin 1999, 19)

Horror Tales

The basic difference between horror tales and tales of the supernatural and other fantastic offerings is that *horror* is a term that describes an affect; a horror story makes its listeners *feel* horror (Clute and Grant 1997). "A 'pure' horror story may occupy the same region as a supernatural fiction—this world is being encroached on by another—but it is shaped *primarily* to convey the affect of horror" (Clute and Grant 1997, 478). These tales are structured so that the teller and the listener are sharing the same reactions, which are evoked by joining the recognition of a threat to one's person or culture with a sense that there is something wrong and monstrous in the invasive presence (Clute and Grant 1997). This fusion is necessary for a tale to be deemed horror. Horror tales are very different from the traditional ghost story. Storyteller Kathryn Windham, a specialist in collecting, writing, and telling ghost stories, said the following:

The stories I tell are not horror stories. There is a vast difference. Horror stories have a lot of blood and guts in them, and you know they really could not have happened. Horror stories talk about people who take off their skins and become other things, or that bleed all over the place, or come after someone with hoods on their arms. Ghost stories, on the other hand, are really rather tender. There's something rather sad and pathetic about many of the ghosts. They are looking for something they love and have lost. Or they are wandering aimlessly. (Unverzagt 1999, 5)

Tales of the Supernatural

Supernatural tales include stories of ghosts, witches, the Devil, vampires, and werewolves, and these stories continue to be popular because people are fascinated by the unknown and the unexplained. Young adults are drawn to stories that shock, frighten, and amaze them while they are safely in their homes, theatres, and classrooms or at the fireside.

A longtime staple of folklore are tales of humans making deals with the Devil for wealth, immortality, power, or the granting of a specific number of wishes. The popularity of these tales revolves around the ingenuity of narrative twists invoked to bring the deals to unexpected conclusions (Clute and Grant 1997). Oddly enough, the idea of such pacts emerged from a medieval cautionary tale about a Bishop Theophilus. The story was later adopted and adapted to justify the persecution of heretics. "All practitioners of witchcraft were assumed to have made such pacts, but theirs tended to be analogous to mere contracts of employment; it was the more grandiose contract made by Faust that became the main prototype of literary pacts" (Clute and Grant 1997, 741). See the "Doctor Faust" entry in the bibliography that follows for a tellable version of his tale.

Ghost Stories

> When I was presenting some of these stories several years ago in a Tokyo high school, a student explained that ghost tales . . . were traditionally recounted on summer nights. "Why?" I asked. "Because," she answered, "summer nights here in Japan are very muggy and very hot. Ghost tales can make you shiver. They give you the chills." (Martin 1996, 3)

The most common type of supernatural story is that of an encounter with a disembodied spirit or persona that is dead—that is, the ghost story. Ghost stories are one of the most frequently told family tales. Usually, with frequent retellings of these family experiences, the teller adopts elements from literary ghost stories to lend action, verisimilitude, and spice.

The function of literary ghost stories has changed over time. During the time of Shakespeare, and reflected in his writing, "the ghost story was seen as a melodramatic warning, a harbinger of doom, or an outward manifestation of an individual's guilt" (Clute and Grant 1997, 403). Later, during the Romantic period of the nineteenth century, gothic fiction became a popular literary form, and the ghost story became the stock-in-trade of the literary output, leading to the extensive use of wailing phantoms, rattling chains, and skeletons and soon reducing the supernatural element to the burlesque. After the Second World War, the renewed interest in spiritualism begat a new generation of ghost story authors and tellers, and this interest has continued to this day. A quick search of the Internet reveals just how many sites are dedicated to the collecting and telling of true occurrences and experiences with a ghost. These stories borrow from both traditions: gothic elements and the melodramatic warnings.

Most storytellers agree that telling sessions for young adults should begin with a ghost story because it will hook the most unwilling listeners and make them receptive to the stories that follow (Horner 1983, 460). The names, places, and dates in ghost stories and contemporary legends may be changed to give the stories more immediacy and verisimilitude. Numerous stories suggested in this chapter, however, are considered actual accounts of supernatural visitations and the facts in these tales should not be tampered with.

The most prevalent ghost stories for young adults are those that reflect great extremes in human experience and are usually told as true happenings. These tales are told either in a way that illustrates just how terrified the storyteller was or nonchalantly to emphasize the courage of the storyteller in frightening circumstances. "Jump tales," the most popular of all the ghost stories, are told to frighten the audience with a startling ending that makes the audience "jump." Jump tales are usually short and precise. When the tale is well told, the teller pulls the audience into the story, and they respond with screams, frightened by the teller's explosive, "You've got it!" at the end of the tale. Often the antagonist of the story is seeking a stolen object, usually a body part such as a toe or a golden arm. The teller leads the character (and the audience) through the hunt—slowly, quietly, and intently—until the suspense is almost unbearable. The teller then quickly points to a member of the audience, exclaiming loudly, "You've got it!" and the audience responds with screams, gasps, and then laughter.

True ghost stories, or supernatural stories that do not come from the literary tradition but are based on anecdotal evidence, are among the most popular types of family stories catalogued at the Smithsonian Institute. Kathryn Windham advises potential tellers of these tales to visit the location of the related experience. "It is important to be very familiar with the facts of the story. Visit cemeteries and check the dates on tombstones to determine that the people in the story really did live and when they died. Check newspaper files for any further information that can enrich the story. Seek out members of the family for their versions of the story" (Unverzagt 1999, 6).

Contemporary Legends

Contemporary legends are "stories that most people have heard as true accounts of real-life experiences" (Brunvand 1981, xi). Developed from incidents and rumors that reflect the fears and anxieties that people have about certain aspects of their lives, contemporary legends often contain elements of suspense and horror. People from all walks of life believe the tales, and publications including *Time, Reader's Digest,* and local newspapers reprint them frequently as true incidents. They are usually known as urban legends, but as I explained in *Tales, Rumors and Gossip,*

Contemporary legends are not folktales; folktales reside within a fictional world and, being told for entertainment, are not believed by the audience (Klintberg 1976, 69). Contemporary legends are not "urban legends" because their settings and narration do not always reflect urban centers. They are not rumor or gossip because they have narrative structure and tell a story.

Contemporary legends are normally considered a subset of the legend genre because legends are narratives that focus on a single episode presented as embarrassing, macabre, miraculous, uncanny, or bizarre. Legends reflect the real world and are told as if they are, or once were, true. The primary function of legends is to inform and reinforce a culture's beliefs and norms, requiring the audience to examine its own worldview. This subset is "contemporary" because its stories reflect the values, concerns, and worldview of today's society expressed in contemporary terms. (de Vos 1996, 4)

These tales are an immediate hook for the young adult audience. Tell the students a contemporary legend and explore both the legends and the society that encourages and fosters the transmission of these tales. When the first edition of *Storytelling for Young Adults* arrived at the scene, teachers and librarians were so fascinated at the possibility of telling and exploring the contemporary tales with young adult audiences, that I soon began to concentrate on researching them for discussion with this target audience. The research grew into the book *Tales, Rumors and Gossip*. Rather than just telling a program of contemporary legends on my visits to schools, I conduct a quasi-workshop about the legends using examples from my book and recent tales circulating on the Internet or in the movie theatres, and telling a tale or two. I may use the same examples in successive presentations, but I make a point of not repeating the tales so that the students have the opportunities to tell their schoolmates the legends they heard. These are highly successful programs, engaging the interests and storytelling abilities of the audience as they agitate to offer the teller the version of the story that they have heard, read, or seen on television programs such as *Freaky Stories* or movies such as *Urban Legends*.

The legends reflect how North American society expects young people and authority figures to behave in times of crisis (Brunvand 1981, 12). Young adults are constantly seeking pertinent information on "proper" behavior and "correct" attitudes that can be explored in safety. Contemporary legends are concerned with violence, horror, threats posed by technology, impurity of food, personal embarrassment, relationships with friends and family, death, the supernatural, and other sources of anxiety (Schwartz 1981, 97). A constant theme of these tales is the young adult leaving home. The tales are cautionary tales, driving home the warning, "Be careful! This could happen to you." Contemporary legends also contain thinly disguised sexual themes that serve as both entertainment and cautionary notices.

Printed contemporary legends vary in length, depending on the amount of embellishment that the author has added to the basic story. Before the easy accessibility of e-mail, oral variants of the tales were filled with localized details that brought each tale close to home, but now they are often forwarded "intact" and the impact of the individual tale has lessened. For a full discussion on contemporary legends and their relationship to literary tales as well as the mass media, I recommend turning to *Tales, Rumors and Gossip* for basic outlines of these tales and references to variants published in collections before 1996. The references for contemporary legends I have in the bibliography that follows are to tales that have been published since 1996 or that were not included in *Tales, Rumors and Gossip*.

Annotated Bibliography

Apparitions

A ghost story is told to the king of Persia in 1816, relating the supernatural adventure of his favorite officer, Marshal Blucher, when he was sixteen years old. Blucher had lost his entire family in the Seven Years' War, and their ghosts revealed their fate to him. They had now, he tells the king, returned to welcome him home again.

> San Souci, Robert D., reteller. 1998. *A Terrifying Taste of Short & Shivery: Thirty Creepy Tales.* New York: Delacorte, pp. 30–34. 4 min. An abridged version of an account that appeared in *Apparitions: A Narrative of Facts* by the Reverend Bourchier Wrey Saville in 1880.

Appointment in Samarra

After making eye-contact with a surprised Death at the marketplace one morning, the man decides to flee the city, hoping to escape what he believes is his fate. Death, however, was only surprised to see him because she knew she was collecting him that evening in a different and faraway city.

> San Souci, Robert D., reteller. 1997. *Even More Short & Shivery: Thirty Spine-Tingling Tales.* New York: Delacorte, pp. 1–4. 3 min. The author states that this is one of the world's best-known stories with numerous variants from around the world. "The Middle Eastern story underscores the folly of trying to escape one's destiny" (149).

Blackbeard

A quick summary of some of the tales and rumors surrounding the life and legacy of pirate Captain Edward Teach, the man known as Blackbeard. There was the attempt to replicate hell and see how long he and his men could tolerate the fumes and heat, as well as the deadly duel between

Blackbeard and Lieutenant Robert Maynard of the Royal Navy. But did the pirate really disappear after his death? If so, who is the headless corpse that is often sighted swimming through the waters of Ocracoke Inlet?

Spencer, Ann. 2001. *Song of the Sea: Myths, Tales and Folklore*. Toronto: Tundra, pp. 144–48. 6 min.

The Buried Treasure

A father of two sons leaves his eldest son everything because his younger son is a spendthrift. Before he dies, the father decrees that the younger son may obtain his inheritance when he learns the value of hard work. To survive, the younger brother goes to work as one of the tenant farmers on his brother's land. Several years later he has a dream of buried treasure, after which he finds a jar of gold ingots. He is an honorable man, and because the gold was found on his brother's land, he informs him of the buried gold. When the brother digs up the jar, he finds it filled with snakes. In his anger, the brother dumps the jar of snakes at his brother's feet, but it is once again filled with gold—the inheritance his father had left for him.

Yep, Laurence. 1995. *Tree of Dreams: Ten Tales from the Garden of Night*. New York: Bridgewater, pp. 75–79. 9 min.

But I'm Not!

A haunted house and five young men trying to prove themselves provide the setting and characters for this jump tale. It offers a lot of blood and gore and the chance to be dramatic.

Young, Richard, and Judy Dockrey Young. 1993. *The Scary Story Reader: Forty-one of the Scariest Stories for Sleepovers, Campfires, Car & Bus Trips—Even for First Dates*. Little Rock, AR: August House, pp. 117–19. 3 min.

The Call from the Grave

A timely storm helps to connect a young girl, left alone when the babysitter becomes stranded, with her beloved grandfather in his grave.

Young, Richard, and Judy Dockrey Young. 1993. *The Scary Story Reader: Forty-one of the Scariest Stories for Sleepovers, Campfires, Car and Bus Trips—Even for First Dates*. Little Rock, AR: August House, pp. 31–33. 4 min.

The Case of the Invisible Passengers

A taxi driver earns three days wages when he takes a woman to the cemetery and waits for her. She returns but not necessarily alone. Two potential zonbi are with her.

Louis, Liliane Nerette. 1999. *When Night Falls, Kric! Krac! Haitian Folktales* (World Folklore Series). Englewood, CO: Libraries Unlimited, 113–14. 2 min. A zonbi is "a dead person who has been brought back to life, or a wandering spirit of a dead person" (182).

Christmas Eve

The story of the blacksmith Vakula, his quest to woo his sweetheart Oksana, his dealings with the Devil, and his saving of the Christmas season.

Husain, Shahrukh, reteller. 1999. *Stories from the Opera*. New York: Barefoot Books, pp. 40–48. 13 min. Based on a short story by the Russian writer, Nikolai Gogol and written as an opera by Nikolai Rimsky-Korsakov. "*Christmas Eve* (1895) almost never reached the stage because the Grand Duke, who watched a dress-rehearsal, was offended that anyone could play the part of the tsarina.. . . Before the opera could be performed, Rimsky-Korsakov had to agree to change the tsarina's part for that of a male courtier" (80).

Death and the Two Friends

George and Aaron have been friends for a long time, but George's patience soon grows thin after Aaron becomes ill. Aaron weakly repeats, "I wish I were dead," until George shouts it out for him to demonstrate the volume he should use to catch Death's attention. Well, Death notices all right. And Aaron, well, he recovers from his illness and lives a long time—but, he's alone now.

San Souci, Robert D., Reteller. 1997. *Even More Short and Shivery: Thirty Spine-Tingling Tales*. New York: Delacorte, pp. 110–12. 4 min. Retold from John Bennett's *Doctor to the Dead: Grotesque Legends and Folk Tales of Old Charleston* (1943).

Doctor Faust

Faust makes a deal with the Devil in order to acquire knowledge and power and agrees with the Devil's demands for his soul. Although he regrets the deal at the final hour, there is no way out.

McCaughrean, Geraldine, reteller. 1997. *The Bronze Cauldron: Myths and Legends of the World*. London: Orion, pp. 31–34. 6 min. "Georgius Sabellious lived in sixteenth-century Germany: a doctor, fortune-teller, astrologer and magician. He roused the anger of the Church, but had several rich and influential clients. After his death, the rumors about him were wild and inventive. 'Faustus Junio' (as he called himself) became the subject of fairground puppet shows" (127).

The Drinking Companions

A friendly farmer makes friends with a young man he meets while fishing in a river. After a year of friendship, the young man discloses that he is a ghost who drowned in that river and will be moving on because he is to be replaced by a new ghost who will drown the following evening. When the ghost discovers his replacement is a young mother with a young child, he saves the mother from drowning and is made a local god some distance away. Before he leaves, he invites his friend to come and visit. The farmer makes the long journey, and when he returns home he becomes rich and comfortable but never forgets the spirits of those who died in the river.

Matthews, John, reteller. 1999. *Giants, Ghosts and Goblins: Traditional Tales from Around the World*. New York: Barefoot Books, pp. 42–49. 9 min. Retold from Moss Robert's *Chinese Fairy Tales and Fantasies* (1979).

Emptying the Granary

When a farmer borrows grain from his neighbor and does not repay the debt, he finds the granary empty the next time he requests a loan.

MacDonald, Margaret Read, reteller. 1999. *Earth Care: World Folktales to Talk About*. North Haven, CT: Linnet, pp. 117. 1 min. MacDonald does not identify the source of this tale other than stating that it is based on a European folktale (155).

The Fiddler

The fiddler is rewarded for his entertaining tunes but the price eventually proves to be much too high. His frenzied fiddling is witnessed on All Hallows' Eve, but there is no redemption for the fiddler of the fairy folk. It is said that the fiddle can still be heard on Halloween for those brave enough to seek the site of the fiddler's final performance.

San Souci, Robert D., Reteller. 1998. *A Terrifying Taste of Short and Shivery: Thirty Creepy Tales*. New York: Delacorte, pp. 15–19. 4 min. Another version can be found in Heather McNeil's *The Celtic Breeze: Stories of the Otherworld from Scotland, Ireland and Wales* (2001) 180–85.

The Flying Dutchman

The experiences of Captain Daland of *The Norwegian* after he meets the ghost of the legendary captain of *The Dutchman*. Daland agrees to arrange a marriage between the ghost captain and his daughter Senta. Unbeknownst to the two of them, Senta is familiar with the ballad and plight of the *Flying Dutchman* and wishes she could be the one to break the spell and set him free from his constant wanderings. Although her friends and family try and dissuade her, Senta does what she has set out to do.

Husain, Shahrukh, reteller. 1999. *Stories from the Opera*. New York: Barefoot Books, pp. 40–48. 13 min. Based on the opera by Richard Wagner.

The Forest

When the woodcutter and his sons ignore the spirits of the trees and the old customs, they soon pay an extreme price for their willfulness.

Spariosu, Milhai I., and Dezso Benedek, retellers. 1994. *Ghosts, Vampires, and Werewolves: Eerie Tales from Transylvania*. New York: Orchard Books, pp. 9–13. 8 min. This tale comes from loggers in the Carpathian Forest in Transylvania. "The Latin word *Transylvania* means 'across, or beyond, the woods,' and in the olden times this land was one vast expanse of virgin forest" (98).

The Ghost Ship

This is the story of Blanche de Beaumont and her fatal encounter with pirates on her voyage from France to the New World. When captured by the pirates and then selected to be the bride of the captain, Blanche threw herself overboard during the wedding ceremony. The other female prisoners followed her lead. Sometime later, the pirate ship shattered against a jagged rock, led there by Blanche's ghostly presence . The rock is now known as Rocher Percee, or Pierced Rock, and the ship, well, it has become a ghost ship, sailing the Gulf of the Saint Lawrence, looking for a safe harbor it will never find.

> Berube, Jocelyn. 1994. In *Next Teller: A Book of Canadian Storytelling*. Collected by Dan Yashinsky. Charlottetown, P.E.I.: Ragweed, pp. 192–96. 6 min.

The Golden Plow

The king sorely missed his advisor Solomon the Wise when Solomon takes a sabbatical and disappears. The king devises a riddle to find Solomon once again.

> MacDonald, Margaret Read, reteller. 1999. *Earth Care: World Folktales to Talk About*. North Haven, CT: Linnet, pp. 86–87. 2 min. Also found in Jean Ure's *Rumanian Folktales* (1960).

The Golden Vanity

The captain of the Golden Vanity accepts the help of a young cabin boy in order to get himself out of difficulty on the high seas. Unfortunately for young Billy, the captain cannot be trusted to live up to his promises.

> McCaughrean, Geraldine, reteller. 1997. *The Bronze Cauldron: Myths and Legends of the World*. London: Orion, pp. 68–70. 5 min. This story is usually sung as a ballad with many versions, the oldest of which names the captain as Sir Walter Raleigh (128).

Golem

Rabbi Loew created the man of clay to protect his people from persecution in the city of Prague during the sixteenth century. After the Golem convinces the attackers to leave the Jewish people alone, the Rabbi causes him to return to clay. The clay is then hidden safely away so that, perhaps, "when the desperate need for justice is united with holy purpose, Golem will come to life once more" (unpaged text).

> Wisniewski, David. 1996. *Golem*. New York: Clarion. 10 min. This award-winning picture book includes historical notes on the Golem. Different rabbis have been credited with the creation of the Golem, but the most famous of all the Golem stories involves the historical figure Rabbi Loew in Prague.

The Hairy Hands

Dismissing the stories of the haunting of the road in Dartmouth, Marjory and Frederick spend the night along the road in their camper. While Frederick sleeps soundly through the night, Marjory experiences terror as the hairy hand attempts to gain entrance into their camper. The terror escalates when Marjory realizes that the stories always spoke of *two* hairy hands!

> San Souci, Robert D., Reteller. 1998. *A Terrifying Taste of Short & Shivery: Thirty Creepy Tales*. New York: Delacorte, pp. 52–57. 4 min. This retelling is based on several written sources, but research shows that although the hairy hands seem to belong to a highwayman, the story itself only began circulating in the second decade of the twentieth century (151).

The Halloween Changeling

Jamie joins in the Halloween celebrations with the fairies as they kidnap a young woman. Jamie falls in love with her and snatches her away from the fairies. They work their magic on her, rendering her deaf and dumb before Jamie's mother can rescue her. The following year, Jamie returns to the fairies and overhears the cure for the young woman's condition and once again tricks the fairies. He and the young woman return to her parents' home, and after convincing them of her identity (a changeling had been left in her place), she and Jamie marry.

> Gilchrist, Cherry, reteller. 1998. *A Calendar of Festivals*. Bristol, UK: Barefoot Books, pp. 45–53. 10 min. Based on Alfred Perceval Graves's *The Irish Fairy Book* and W. B. Yeats's *A Treasury of Irish Myth, Legend and Folklore*.

Island of the Lost Children

A griffin snatches Prince Hagen away from his family, but the boy escapes from the griffin's nest and is deposited on a deserted island. He discovers three maidens who had been hiding from the griffins for several years. They live together until a drowned warrior washes to shore. Hagen puts on the warrior's armor and sword and is immediately attacked by the griffins, whom he valiantly defeats. A passing ship eventually rescues the children. Hagen arranges his homecoming to satisfy the captain of the ship who has sworn vengeance against Hagen's father. All ends well: the family is reunited, the captain is rewarded, and Hagen marries one of the maidens.

> Osborne, Mary Pope, reteller. 1998. *Favorite Medieval Tales*. New York: Scholastic, pp. 25–33. 11 min. Retold from the thirteenth-century German poem "Gundrun."

Ivon Tortik

An ugly young hunchback wishes to marry the beautiful daughter of the richest miller in all of Brittany. She laughs at his suit and tells him she will only marry him only if he is handsome, has a straight back, and has pockets full of gold pieces. He sets off to acquire these things. On All Hallow's Eve, he dances with the fairy folk and helps them with an ancient song, and they reward him with a handsome countenance and a straight back. He continues on his quest until Christmas Eve, when he overhears two crows divulging the secret of the giant standing stones. His etching of a Christmas star on one of the stones saves his life and allows him to gather sufficient gold to return home and marry his sweetheart. The fallen stone, still carrying Ivon's carving, can be seen in Brittany to this day.

Kane, Alice, reteller. 1995. *The Dreamer Awakes.* Peterborough, ON: Broadview Press, pp. 21–29. 10 min. From Jacques Dorey's *Three and the Moon: Legendary Stories of Old Brittany, Normandy and Provence* (1929).

Jealous Vampire

When the beautiful young maiden is courted by the vampire, she does not know how to resist his advances. The wise old woman of the village gives her advice, but before she can put the advice to use, the young girl is responsible for the death of all her family and her own murder. Later, when a beautiful flower is spotted and picked by a handsome young man, the wisdom of the old woman's advice comes to bloom. This is a strange but romantic tale.

Spariosu, Milhai I., and Dezso Benedek, Retellers. 1994. *Ghosts, Vampires, and Werewolves: Eerie Tales from Transylvania.* New York: Orchard Books, pp. 20–25. 8 min. Heard from an old Gypsy peddler, this is a popular tale with many versions in Transylvania.

Keep Your Secrets

A young bride, while talking to her husband, is overheard and cautioned by her mother not to tell all her secrets. She follows her mother's sage advice and, because she has not revealed everything, manages to escape from the evil being whom she unknowingly married.

Carter, Angela, editor. 1990. *The Old Wives' Fairy Tale Book.* New York: Pantheon Fairy Tale and Folklore Library, pp. 64–65. 4 min. From *Tales Told in Togoland* (1931), 213. Carter says of this story, "The witch duel, or duel of transformations, commemorated in the European children's game 'Scissors, paper, stone,' is a recurring phenomenon amongst supernatural beings" (235). She also notes that this is the best of all "Mother knows best" stories!

The King's Dragon

A silly tale that plays with puns (Dragon and Dragoons) and the opening segment of the traditional tale "Stone Soup."

Yolen, Jane. 1993. *Here There Be Dragons.* San Diego, CA: Harcourt Brace, pp. 84–86. 4 min. The story was written to be performed on stage.

Lullaby

A solitary train traveler finds that he has suddenly been joined by a young woman singing a lullaby to the bundle she is rocking in her arms. He tries to ignore her, but his curiosity gets the better of him and he tries to get a better look at the woman and her bundle. As he moves forward, there is a terrible crash, and he is rendered unconscious. When he comes to, the conductor informs him that he has been alone the whole time. The woman, he subsequently discovers, is a warning ghost who comes at times of danger to the train. She always returns to the place where her new bridegroom had his head cut off in a freak accident.

> San Souci, Robert D., reteller. 1997. *Even More Short and Shivery: Thirty Spine-Tingling Tales*. New York: Delacorte, pp. 105–109. 8 min. Adapted from *Lord Halifax's Ghost Book* (1936). Lord Halifax insisted the story was true: "he heard it from the nephew of the man who actually had the experience" (158).

Ma Yarwood's Wedding Ring

When the stranger came to town and saw the wedding ring on Mrs. Yarwood's finger, he just had to have it, even if it meant breaking into her house and murdering her—and that's just what he did. Ma Yarwood really valued her ring, however, so she came back from the dead to recover it.

> Cox, Rita. 1997. In *Ghostwise: A Book of Midnight Stories* collected by Dan Yashinsky. Charlottetown, P.E.I.: Ragweed, pp. 123–27. 6 min. "There was an old house outside St. Joseph's in Trinidad. The people say it's haunted. My Aunt Jane told me 'The Wedding Ring' about the house" (210),

Macie and Boo Hag

This tale is a first-person account of a young woman named Macie, who was ridden by a boo-hag for several nights and how Macie's mother caught the hag and imprisoned her. Unfortunately, the teller concludes, people today do not know how to get rid of boo hags!

> Hamilton, Virginia. 1995. *Her Stories: African American Folktales, Fairy Tales and True Tales*. New York: Blue Sky, pp. 51–55. 5 min. Collected by Chalmers S. Murray for the South Carolina Writer's Project, 1935–1941; informant unknown.

The Magic Gifts

Leo left his home to find work to help support himself and his father. He started working for a farmer and stayed several years. When he finally left, the farmer gave him a magic hat that rendered the wearer invisible, a fiddle that made everyone dance, and a gun that never missed its mark. These three gifts were used wisely to help make Leo's fortune, and when he returned home, his father recognized the most valuable gift of all: the growth of his son from a boy to a man.

Reneaux, J. J., reteller. 1994. In *Ready-to-Tell Tales: Sure-Fire Stories from America's Favorite Storytellers*. Edited by David Holt and Bill Mooney. Little Rock, AR: August House, pp. 69–73. 5 min.

Mrs. Number Three

Chao stayed at Mrs. Number Three's inn but did not partake of the wine as the other guests did. He alone was the witness to the baking of the magic buckwheat cakes that were to be their morning repast. When each guest ate a cake, he or she was transformed into a donkey. Only Chao escaped this fate. On his return journey, he substituted his own cakes for those of his hostess and tricked her into ingesting one of her own. She proved to be a strong and reliable donkey for four years until someone recognized her and set her free. She was never seen again.

Carter, Angela, editor. 1990. *The Old Wives' Fairy Tale Book*. New York: Pantheon Fairy Tale and Folklore Library, pp. 64–65. 4 min. From G. Willoughby-Meade's *Chinese Ghouls and Goblins* (1928) 191. Carter compares this tale with that of Apuleius's *The Golden Ass* and with Circe, the enchantress in Homer's *Odyssey* who transformed her clients into swine. (See also the entry for "A Night of Terror.")

The Murky Secret

A bottle filled with a murky liquid joins the bottle containing a pickled mermaid on a shelf at the local drugstore. When a fierce storm hits the town, the townspeople decide that it is the wrath of the merfolk and demand the mermaid be returned to the sea. Although the druggist shows them that the mermaid was a trick, the crowd is even more upset and attacks the drugstore. The druggist hands the second bottle over to a young boy for safekeeping, but the boy frees the contents: a real mermaid. Much later, that same bottle washes up to shore, no longer containing a mermaid, but the shrunken corpse of the druggist.

Olson, Arielle North, and Howard Schwartz, retellers. 1999. *Ask the Bones: Scary Stories from Around the World*. New York: Viking, pp. 10–16. 13 min. From John Bennett's *The Doctor to the Dead: Grotesque Legends and Folk Tales of Old Charleston* (1946).

Narrow Escape

A retelling of the urban legend "A Killer in the Back Seat."

San Souci, Robert D., reteller. 1998. *A Terrifying Taste of Short and Shivery: Thirty Creepy Tales*. New York: Delacorte, pp. 130–36. 6 min.

Never Far From You

At their wedding celebration, a young couple decide to play games with their guests. The last game they decide to play is "hide-and-seek." When the young bride is not found, the despondent groom remains close to her last known location, his home, and lives a long life of sorrow. Just before he passes on, he learns that his young bride was never far from him at all!

> San Souci, Robert D., reteller. 1997. *Even More Short and Shivery: Thirty Spine-Tingling Tales*. New York: Delacorte, pp. 52–56. 5 min. A prose rendition of a tale made popular by Thomas Haynes Bayley's ballad "The Mistletoe Bough."

A Night of Terror

Two students find themselves taking shelter with two women who they soon discover are witches. While feigning sleep, the men discover that the witches have transformed other travelers into oxen who, when back in their human forms, perform all the witches' household tasks. The students realize that it is the food that causes the transformations and refuse to eat. The witches force them to take bread with them as they leave and send their fierce dogs after them. The students throw the bread at the dogs that race back to the cottage. After hearing fierce bellowing and hysterical barking, the two men see the oxen running after them. They decide to take off the halters to turn the oxen back to men, but unfortunately for the students, the oxen are not what they seem. A truly disturbing tale.

> Olson, Arielle North, and Howard Schwartz, retellers. 1999. *Ask the Bones: Scary Stories from Around the World*. New York: Viking, pp. 60–65. 11 min. From Joseph Dan's *Ha-Sippur ha-Hasisi* (The Hasidic Story), 1975. (See also the entry for "Mrs. Number Three.")

A Night of Terrors

Mary Jo is not feeling very well; she is pleased that her housemate Linda is going out that evening so that she can sleep and not be disturbed. Mary Jo has her dog to keep her company. She keeps drifting in and out of sleep, disturbed by strange noises, but is reassured when her dog licks her hand from under the bed. But things are not all that they seem to be! One version of a tale that is very popular with young teens.

> San Souci, Robert D., reteller. 1997. *Even More Short and Shivery: Thirty Spine-Tingling Tales*. New York: Delacorte, pp. 128–35. 10 min. A reworking and blending of the contemporary legends, "The Licked Hand" and "The Roommate's Death."

One Ox, Two Ox, Three Ox, and the Dragon King

Three brothers—named One Ox, Two Ox, and Three Ox—travel separately to the cave of the Dragon King to fetch the Waters of Life to save their mother's life. One Ox's adventures net him a magic horse, Two Ox is rewarded with a magic hairpin, and Three Ox discovers how to make himself invisible. The three brothers meet and travel together to defeat the Dragon King. Although this is a fairly long tale to tell, the individual episodes can be told as a serial story.

Yolen, Jane. 1993. *Here There Be Dragons*. San Diego, CA: Harcourt Brace, pp. 118–47. 26 min. Yolen says that although she has used many elements from Chinese mythology, this is not a Chinese tale. "The solution to the Ox brothers' problem is entirely Western and influenced by the many fairy tales from European sources that I have read over the years" (118).

The Peach-Blossom Forest

A poor fisherman follows a whim to investigate a grove of peach trees he had never seen before. Two young women, dressed in the fashion of the distant past, invite him to join their picnic. They introduce him to their father, who tells the fisherman he must leave and not tell anyone of this wondrous home that has been hidden for 500 years. The people are serene, happy, and peaceful, and no one knows how to find them. The fisherman promises to keep quiet, although he knows in his heart that he will not be able to keep his promise. When he returns to the area to show officials this wonderful place, it has completely vanished.

Kane, Alice, reteller. 1995. *The Dreamer Awakes*. Peterborough, ON: Broadview Press, pp. 93-97. 4 min. The story was originally an essay written by the Chinese poet Tao Yuanming (365–427), who lived in a period of corruption, disunity, and despair. "This piece, which depicts a Taoist utopia with Taoist goddesses—though in Alice Kane's version their names are the sort that would have been given to bondmaids—is one of the works that every educated Chinese used to read when being trained in literature. The simple statement of a longing for sanity and sanctuary carried two-thousand-year-old memories of the peach tree that stands in Chinese myth as the doorway to the spirit world. To this day, the gift of peaches expresses a wish for long life" (177). Adapted from Jo Manton and Robert Gittings's *The Peach-Blossom Forest and Other Chinese Legends* (1951).

Peacock's Ghost

When John Peacock went looking for the farm that he had inherited, he found much more than he had been looking for! A truly scary tale.

San Souci, Robert D., reteller. 1998. *A Terrifying Taste of Short and Shivery: Thirty Creepy Tales*. New York: Delacorte, pp. 109–113. 4 min. Adapted from the narrative "Louisiana Ghost Story" originally printed in *Journal of American Folklore* 12 (1899). The author says, "I have kept the thrust and language of the original tale, which is essentially the old woman's story. But I created the contemporary framing story, and held back the fact that the ghost is *female,* for an extra impact at the end" (156).

Phantom (Revenant)

The ghost in the haunted house in Haiti is not fearsome, yet no one can stay more than one night in the house until a visiting priest discovers the revenant's purpose.

Louis, Liliane Nerette. 1999. *When Night Falls, Kric! Krac! Haitian Folktales,* World Folklore series. Englewood, CO: Libraries Unlimited, 125–27. 5 min.

Police Report

The eyewitness report from one of the participants in a Halloween visit to the cemetery and the marble tombstone of Agnes Doubleday. The teens were frightened by the ghostly apparition that demanded they get off her stone. A surprise ending to a literary working of a legend-tripping episode.

Yolen, Jane. 1998. *Here There Be Ghosts*. San Diego, CA: Harcourt Brace, pp. 22–26. 9 min. Jane Yolen says that one of the threads for this literary folktale is the fact that she and her friends, when they were teenagers, would picnic on the marble tombstone of someone named Agnes (22).

Prom Ghost

Thom, the narrator of the story, lost her brother and his girlfriend in a car accident on the night of the junior prom five years before. Their restless ghosts made their presence known around the school, but it isn't until Thom's sister attends her first prom that the ghosts become extremely active. A literary tale to scare anyone!

Yolen, Jane. 1998. *Here There Be Ghosts*. Orlando, FL: Harcourt Brace, pp. 110–20. 16 min.

The Rosewood Bed

At a party in a recently renovated home in Vancouver, British Columbia, the hosts and guests are visited by the appearance of a dying woman and her smirking husband in a large four-poster bed made of rosewood. The ghosts quickly fade, but the hosts decide to sell the house. When the newly laid carpet is examined during the sale, a more tangible sign of the visitation is discovered.

MacDonald, Margaret Read, reteller. 1995. *Ghost Stories from the Pacific Northwest*. Little Rock, AR: August House, pp. 41–42. 2 min. From Sheila Harvey's *Some Canadian Ghosts* and newspaper reports published in *The Province* by Greg McIntyre.

A Snap of the Fingers

Miguel is curious and disregards his grandfather's advice to stay away from the old soldier and his raven, El Diablo. Miguel sees firsthand the nature of the soldier's power and struggles to resist it. But it's very difficult to resist temptation when all you have to do is snap your fingers to have all the wealth and power you want. The price Miguel will have to pay is something beyond consideration. Or is it?

San Souci, Robert D., reteller. 1998. *A Terrifying Taste of Short and Shivery: Thirty Creepy Tales*. New York: Delacorte, pp. 123–29. 6 min. Based on the story, "The Calle de Puente del Cuervo" ("The Street of the Bridge of the Raven") in Thomas A. Janvier's *Legends of the City of Mexico* (1910).

The Snoring Ghost

In 1912, a family moves to Vancouver Island from the mainland of British Columbia. They reside in a farmer's shack while their new home is being built. From one of the bedrooms the family can hear loud snoring from downstairs. They examine the shack but cannot find the source of the noise that can only be heard in that one room. The arrival of a friend six weeks later quiets the ghost, but it returns to haunt the next inhabitant of the shack. No one ever discovered who (or what) it was.

MacDonald, Margaret Read, reteller. 1995. *Ghost Stories from the Pacific Northwest.* Little Rock, AR: August House, pp. 66–69. 5 min. From Margery Wighton's article published in the *Vancouver Sun* (1952).

Souls

The people around him teach the boy that insects, worms, kittens, and "undesirables" such as minorities and handicapped people have no soul and therefore will not go to heaven. He had no remorse about disposing of them until one day a giant hand descends from the sky, and, saying that because he has never demonstrated that he has a soul himself, disposes of him the same way.

Yolen, Jane. 1998. *Here There Be Ghosts.* Orlando: Harcourt Brace, pp. 95–98. 5 min. Jane Yolen's editor contends that this tale is "the most frightening ghost story imaginable" (95).

Special Delivery

A gruesome tale of murder and revenge results when a young man's father refuses to let him marry the girl of his choice. Years later, the postman is asked to deliver the one thing that will lay the young man's ghost to rest.

Spariosu, Milhai I., and Dezso Benedek, retellers. 1994. *Ghosts, Vampires, and Werewolves: Eerie Tales from Transylvania.* New York: Orchard Books, pp. 26–36. 10 min. The author heard this tale from an old Saxon shoemaker. The Saxons settled in southern Transylvania and brought their legends and ghosts to their new home.

The Story of the Green Lady

A woman goes upstairs to rest during a party and is frightened by the ghost of a green lady. The ghost was known to appear as a warning of imminent death and, as predicted, two weeks later, the woman falls ill and dies.

MacDonald, Margaret Read, reteller. 1995. *Ghost Stories from the Pacific Northwest.* Little Rock, AR: August House, pp. 60–61. 4 min. From an interview with Jenny Alexander.

Tam Lin

Marillier reworks the traditional Scottish ballad as part of her novel. Tom is an enchanted young man who is rescued from the Faerie Queen by his mortal lover, Janet. This is a hard-won battle but Janet has the courage and love to be victorious. This ballad and its contemporary reworkings are explored in chapter 3 of Altmann and de Vos's book, *Tales, Then and Now*.

> Marillier, Juliet. 2001. *Son of Shadows*. New York: TOR, pp. 137–41. 10 min.

Tod House Ghost Laid

In 1851, John Tod, a Hudson Bay Company chief trader, built one of the first homes of milled lumber in Victoria. The house's reputation as being haunted was well established by the time the Evans family purchased it in 1944. They lived somewhat peacefully with ghostly pranks until two visitors reported the sight of an Indian woman in fetters in the guest bedroom. Research revealed that one of Tod's wives, a native woman, had gone mad and was kept in chains in that room. After that sighting, the ghost became more visible and more destructive until a house renovation unearthed a skeleton. There were no more visitations after that time. The house was declared a historical landmark in 1974 and is no longer haunted by a ghost, just the past (107).

> MacDonald, Margaret Read, reteller. 1995. *Ghost Stories from the Pacific Northwest*. Little Rock, AR: August House, pp. 103–107. 6 min. From several local newspaper stories in the Victoria, British Columbia, area.

The Two Witches

After two witches make a bet, the loser is turned into horse. The winner sells the horse, warning the new owner that the horse's halter must remain on at all times. The owner takes the horse to the river, where a boy removes the halter so it can drink. The horse immediately turns into a fish and swims away. The witch who had cast the spell witnesses the transformation and, taking the form of a hawk, sets out to chase the fish. One witch becomes a songbird for an ailing princess, but the second quickly appears as a doctor, demanding the bird in exchange for helping the princess. The two witches, in various forms, continue their chase until one is fatally defeated.

> Philip, Neil, editor 1999. *Stockings of Buttermilk*. New York: Clarion, pp. 27–28. 2 min. Taken from Helen Zunser's " A New Mexican Village," *Journal of American Folk-Lore* (1935). Philip has given the story a new ending because the original "forgets all about the princess and instead visits a violent death on the coyote" (114).

Vasilisa the Beautiful

Vasilisa has the doll her dead mother gave her to provide comfort and company in the face of her stepmother and stepsister's wrath. It is the doll that guides her and comes to her aids at the house of the fierce witch, Baba Yaga. And it is the doll, too, that makes it possible for Vasilisa to become the beloved bride of the tsar. A frightening tale with a powerful message about kindness.

> Evetts-Secker, Josephine, reteller. 1996. *Mother and Daughter Tales*. London: Barefoot Books, pp. 30–39. 12 min.

Water Wraiths

Water wraiths were thought to be evil omens, harbingers of death and disaster. Not so the water wraith of Sable Island, off the coast of Nova Scotia. This particular water wraith would leave his watery grave to help row the rescue rowboats; once the rescue was done, he would return to the sea to await the next person in need.

> Spencer, Ann. 2001. *Song of the Sea: Myths, Tales and Folklore*. Toronto: Tundra, pp. 161–64. 5 min.

White Cross

When a distraught widow makes selfish demands on her remaining children, she does not realize the lengths her son will go to in order to fulfill her requests. The villagers placed a white cross on her son's grave, finally allowing him rest.

> Spariosu, Milhai I., and Dezso Benedek, retellers. 1994. *Ghosts, Vampires, and Were-wolves: Eerie Tales from Transylvania*. New York: Orchard Books, pp. 3–8. 8 min. This tale is based on an old legend that one of the authors heard about an ancient wooden cross outside his great-uncle's home. "The village people believe that sometimes unhappy people cannot rest in their graves and will haunt the scene of their past misfortunes" (98).

The White Lady of the Seventh Tee

The "white lady" of the Victoria golf course is a famous destination for legend-tripping teenagers. The ghostly sightings were first recorded in the 1940s when the body of Doris Gravlin was discovered near the seventh tee. Her estranged husband, who was thought to have done the deed, was soon found drowned in the ocean. MacDonald's story includes several sightings of the white lady.

> MacDonald, Margaret Read, reteller. 1995. *Ghost Stories from the Pacific Northwest*. Little Rock, AR: August House, pp. 153–56. 6 min. From several local newspaper stories in the Victoria, British Columbia, area.

The Wind Rider

The magician, foiled in his attempt to win the favor of Krystyna, casts a spell on her chosen mate, Andrusz, who finds himself forever flying on the wind until Krystyna sees him and brings him down. Once Krystyna rescues him, they both go the witch Zophia to help them defeat the magician. Zophia gives the magician a taste of his own medicine. Perhaps it is not such a good idea to look up into the eye of a windstorm!

> San Souci, Robert D., reteller. 1997. *Even More Short and Shivery: Thirty Spine-Tingling Tales*. New York: Delacorte, pp. 5256. 8 min. Adapted from "The Wind Rider" in *Folklore and Legend: Russian and Polish* by C. J.

References

Brunvand, Jan Harold. 1981. *The Vanishing Hitchhiker: American Urban Legends and Their Meanings*. New York: W.W. Norton.

Clute, John, and John Grant, ed. 1997. *The Encyclopaedia of Fantasy*. London: Orbit.

de Vos, Gail. 1996. *Tales, Rumors and Gossip: Exploring Contemporary Legends in Grades 7–12*. Littleton, CO: Libraries Unlimited.

Horner, Beth. 1983. "To Tell or Not to Tell: Storytelling for Young Adults." *Illinois Libraries* 65(7): 458–64.

Kevin, Jim. 1999. Scary Stories: Information for Tellers. S*torytelling World* 16 (summer/fall): 13–25.

Klintberg, Bengt af. 1976. Folksagner I dag. *Fataburen* 69–89.

Martin, Rafe, reteller. 1996. *Mysterious Tales of Japan*. New York: G.P. Putnam's Sons.

Schwartz, Alvin. 1981. *Scary Stories to Tell in the Dark*. New York: J.B. Lippincott.

Unverzagt, Kathy. 1999. Kathryn Windham: The "Ghost Lady." An Interview. *Storytelling World* 16 (summer/fall): 4–6.

Chapter 4

Tales of the Folk

> She had a wealth of stories, each connected with the other in intricate and surprising ways. She started out in one story and ended up in another. She pulled up one story, and several others came attached, the way hooks on hangers became caught on one another, so that you reach for one and several come away.
>
> —Michael Bedard, *Stained Glass*

"Most storytellers rely on the traditional narrative material found in folklore, because of its timelessness, antiquity and capacity to elicit laughter, tears or bravos" (de Wit 1979, ix). Because these tales can be understood on a number of levels at once, they appeal to a broad spectrum of the population.

Folktales and the Young Adult

Most of tales that I tell to young adult audiences are folktales. I am particularly fond of stories with strong female characters (I have daughters), Jewish tales from my own heritage, and stories of tricksters and twisted endings. I advise students to look to their own cultural heritage first when looking for stories to learn because these tales often speak to us and are easier to learn. The stories in this section appeal to young adults on many levels and may be told for a variety of reasons, the first and foremost being entertainment, I hope. One of the other basic incentives for telling folktales to young adults is that these stories are usually about people their age who are leaving home for the first time, finding a job, a mate, and a future. When you look carefully at the body of folktales, you soon discover that few of the protagonists of these tales are young children. In fact, they are usually teenagers, or they would have been considered teenagers, if the concept had been invented at the time the tales were first told. There are, of course, folktales that are populated with older characters as protagonists. These tales are not usually as successful with the young adult audience. The vast majority of folktales, however, resonate with young adults because they mirror, to some degree, the psychological and physical changes the young adults are experiencing themselves.

These tales may not be all that familiar. I have deliberately included less-well-known tales. One of the sad things that I notice when telling stories in schools is that many young audiences are no longer aquainted with a wide body of folktales. If they know any, the tales are always the same few: "Beauty and the Beast," "Cinderella," "Goldilocks and the Three Bears," "Hansel and Gretel," "Jack and the Beanstalk," "The Little Mermaid," "Little Red Riding Hood," "The Princess and the Pea," "Rapunzel," "Rumpelstiltskin," "Sleeping Beauty," "Snow White," "The Three Pigs," and "The Ugly Duckling." These folktales come from collections of German tales collected by the Grimm brothers, French tales rewritten for royalty by Perrault, and from the imagination of Hans Christian Andersen.

Of the large possible number of tales available in books today, it is regrettable to say that the same few tales are repeated over and over again (and purchased over and over again). This was brought home vividly to me several years ago at a bookstore. A proud, new grandmother was browsing the shelves for a collection of fairy tales for the new grandchild. Delighted with her enthusiasm, I, as a fellow customer, began to show her the best collections of tales for young children. The woman looked at the contents and discarded any books that contained tales that were not absolutely familiar to her. The collection she eventually purchased contained only eight tales, all of them contained in the list I cited in the previous paragraph, and she was pleased with this selection. Before she left, she thanked me for my help, looked at me oddly, and said, "If those other fairy tales were any good, I would have heard of them."

The reception of folktales in the Western world today (and to a great extent throughout the entire world) has been heavily influenced by the animated film versions of the most well-known tales produced by the Walt Disney studios and by the mass-market books that derive from them. Young adults have preconceived notions of what a tale should be and for whom the tale is intended. It is one of the responsibilities of the storyteller to alter these preconceptions.

The mass-mediated fairy tales have a technologically produced universal voice and image which impose themselves on the imagination of passive audiences . . . The original tale was cultivated by a narrator and the audience to clarify and interpret phenomena in a way that would strengthen meaningful social bonds. . . . The [mass-media] narrative is no longer responsive to an active audience but manipulates it according to the vested interests of the state and private industry. (Zipes 1979, 17)

To investigate further the influences of the Disney studio on the tales "Snow White" and "The Little Mermaid," please see the discussion in *New Tales for Old* and *Tales, Then and Now*, coauthored by Anna Altmann and me. Both of these volumes discuss the changes made to most of the famous tales throughout time.

Folktales and Fairy Tales Defined

Historically, fairy tales and folktales gave vent to the frustrations of the common folk and united the members of a community. The two terms, *fairy tale* and *folktale*, are used interchangeably today, but technically there are differences. Both are traditional types of stories that have formulaic language and structure, supernatural motifs, and sympathy for the underdog or commoner. The tales reveal, in an entertaining and enlightening way, the foibles and strengths of mankind. Fairy tales were originally cultivated by upper-class Europeans to ensure that their young people would be properly groomed for their social functions (Zipes 1983, 14). Folktales, on the other hand, were transmitted to the children of upper-class parents through the servants employed within the homes. The tales passed on the mores and standards of the common people and their challenges against people in authority.

Mary Beth Stein, in her entry on folklore and fairy tales in *The Oxford Companion to Fairy Tales*, differentiates the two terms in this way:

The words fairy tale can refer to both a category of oral folk tale and a genre of prose literature. As a term, it is often used by folk narrative scholars when referring specifically to "magic tales," or tales listed under tale-type numbers 300–749 in the Aarne-Thompson tale-type index. The term folk tale is reserved for any tale deriving from or existing in oral tradition and is generally preferred by folklorists and anthropologists. Literary scholars tend to use the [term] fairy tale to refer to a genre of prose literature, which may or may not be based on oral tradition. (167)

To my mind, however, fairy tales refer to a subset of folklore that involve the little people, such as faeries and leprechauns, and that is how I use the term in this volume. I do not further distinguish the two types of tales in this chapter.

Storr defines folktales as "myths of the struggle to become human, to attain a unique identity, and to attain the stature of an individual" (Storr 1986, 66). The majority of folktales are not overly concerned with either the very young or the elderly because "it is the business of these young [characters] to discover who they are; to get away from their parents, to shake off the cloak of family identity and to find their own." Problems in the tales test the character of the protagonists and illuminate possibilities for attaining personal autonomy and social freedom. The tales are a comment on personal and social questions that still concern the young adult today: how couples conduct their relationships and how young people set about solving dilemmas perplexing to themselves or the community (Phelps 1978, viii). The stories stress the need and the right to grow beyond parental decisions and consent. They depict the young adult's necessary growth from a "yes man" to parents and other authority figures into an adult in possession of self-trust and self-knowledge (Shannon 1981, 34).

Folktales are also bearers of cultural archetypes. Archetypes are "subconscious images, ideas, or patterns of thought universally present in memory in all individuals within a race" (Livo and Rietz 1986, 16). They are tools that can be used, through storytelling, to expand and extend human knowledge and awareness. Archetypes aid young adults first in recognizing in themselves and others the capacities for such universal behavior; and second, identifying such behavior when they meet it (Livo and Rietz 1986, 17).

Perception of Folktales

There has long been a disagreement among educators about the value of folktales for today's audiences. The cruel stepmother, the passive princess, and the "happily ever after" endings are three recurring themes that have received negative attention. Storytellers have a responsibility not to portray stepmothers, as a group, as totally negative: if a "cruel stepmother" story must be told, then the program should be balanced with a story involving a positive stepmother character. The same is true of stories involving the elderly, particularly older women. A quick look at the Disney studio portrayals of older women in their film versions of tales shows how elderly women are perceived today: if they are powerful, they are also evil!

Young women are sometimes depicted in the tales in "a dormant or passive state in order to indicate that between the onset of puberty and the time of marriage and motherhood there needed to be a quiet period of growth" (Moran 1987, 21). Moran feels that young adults should be told how passive princess stories served the crucial function of preparing young girls to endure whatever came their way because they were not to take an active part in molding their own destinies (Moran 1987, 22). Others have felt that because men collected and published the tales, the only stories that saw the printed page were ones that comfortably fit into the socializing agendas of the time. Nonetheless, stories featuring positive female roles were always told and are, once again, coming to the forefront as more and more recent publications featuring collections of traditional folktales with strong female characters are being offered. Stories today can help to form a girl or young woman's consciousness of herself as a strong, vital person ready to undertake the challenges that will come her way. This is equally as important for the boys and young men in the audience. Several stories recommended in this book can be found in Kathleen Ragan's (1998) anthology *Fearless Girls, Wise Women and Beloved Sisters*. This collection is a treasure trove of stories from more than seventy countries and cultures and, as the author explains, includes heroines in all stages of life and with all kinds of characteristics (Ragan, n.d.).

There are other types of folktales, such as those that present male characters as sensitive human beings, that have not been as prevalent in the past but are now receiving renewed interest from storytellers, educators, and parents. They are more difficult to pinpoint than those of strong female protagonists because editors and retellers have not focused on these tales at all. Stories containing good masculine roles can be found, however, in many of the tales involving the youngest son in a trio of adventurers. A comparison of the younger son's positive traits with his greedy, inconsiderate brothers is inherent in this type of tale.

The dream of living "happily ever after" has always been a fantasy. Storytellers have an opportunity for helping young adults look for a more realistic vision of the future. They can do this by either leaving off the "happily ever after" or slightly altering the formulaic wording of the ending. "Young people of today, both boys and girls, need to be convinced that they must take their own lives seriously; that there will be helpers along the way, but no rescuers" (Moran 1986, 21). Ragan (n.d.) states that all of the stories in her collection have happy endings on request for one of her daughters. "You'll find a lot of people living happily ever after. Folktales aren't just stories for kids. They present real problems. Then ideas flow without anyone there to veto every improbable suggestion. With consistently happy endings, fairy tales carry the utopian message: Believe that you can better your situation, use your head, you can do it!"

I have long maintained that well-known folktales should not be told to young adults because the tales will be too recognizable as childhood relics; I suggest tellers avoid beginning a story with "once upon a time" for the same reason. I have found that young adult audiences, however, are fascinated by the changes made to the tales that they think they know so well. Although I don't tell these familiar tales in their entirety, I do talk about the changes made to them by various hands throughout the print and film histories of the tales. The result is that audience members frequently swarm the library shelves wanting to find the traditional tellings of these often gruesome tales. (Well, I often make a point of mentioning that gruesome elements exist because that tends to ignite additional interest among this age group.)

Annotated Bibliography

The Blazing Rice Fields
When a respected old farmer lights the village's rice fields ablaze, the horrified and angry people rush to the scene. While they are in the field trying to control the blaze, a huge wave washes over their village, destroying everything. They realize that the old man's seemingly senseless act has saved all their lives.

> Hamilton, Martha, and Mitch Weiss, retellers. 2001. *Through the Grapevine: World Tales Kids Can Read and Tell.* Little Rock, AR: August House, pp. 73–75. 3 min. Retold from Lafcadio Hearn's *Gleanings in Buddha Fields* (1897) and Sara Cone Bryant's *How to Tell Stories to Children* (1924).

Clever Anaeet
When Prince Vachagan falls in love and offers marriage to Anaeet, a clever peasant girl, she refuses his proposal until he has a trade. He becomes a weaver and years after their wedding dons the disguise of a peasant, leaving his wife in charge of the kingdom, to discover the reason for the disappearance of so many of his people. He is captured but convinces his captors to let him weave a carpet that is then sent to Queen Anaeet. Unbeknownst to his captors, Vachagan has woven a message into the carpet and is rescued—all because Anaeet insisted that everyone should have a trade, even a prince. Kathleen Ragan comments that Anaeet "knows that he will be a good partner in life because he is a man who knows how to listen to a woman" (Ragan, 91).

> Batt, Tanya Robyn, reteller. 2000. *The Fabrics of Fairytale: Stories Spun from Far and Wide.* New York: Barefoot Books, pp. 10–16. 11 min. Another fine version of this story can be found in Kathleen Ragan's *Fearless Girls, Wise Women, and Beloved Sisters*, pp. 81–91. A lovely picture book version is also available: *A Weave of Words*, retold by Robert D. San Souci and illustrated by Raul Colon (New York: Orchard Books, 1998).

Clever Marcela
When the king sets a series of tests for a clever peasant girl named Marcela, she passes them with flying colors. She is as impressed with the ingenuity of his tests as he is with her answers, so when he asks her to marry him, she readily agrees. Her cleverness almost ends the relationship, but the king realizes that a clever wife is not only an asset but also a necessity. A fresh retelling of a popular tale.

Tchana, Katrin. 2000. *The Serpent Slayer and Other Stories of Strong Women.* Boston: Little, Brown, pp. 19–23. 8 min.

The Couple's Journey

Following the advice of her beloved grandfather, the young Omuskego woman marries the stranger who has come to the tribe's summer gathering place. She follows him on a long journey to his homeland in return for his promise that they would keep her language alive and that he would take her back to her people one day. He keeps both promises, and this is why "Cree came to be the language of some of the people of the mountains" (49).

Andrews, Jan, reteller. 2000. *Out of the Everywhere: Tales for a New World.* Toronto: Groundwood, pp. 43–49. 8 min. The author heard this tale from Omushkego elder Penishish—Louis Bird.

The Crafty Woman

The Devil cannot tolerate the happiness and contentment of the young couple, yet he cannot seem to make them quarrel. A shoeless old woman makes a deal with him to gain footwear, and with a couple of well-placed false warnings, she defeats the Devil at his own game.

Carter, Angela, ed. 1992. *The Second Virago Book of Fairy Tales.* London: Virago Press, pp. 44–45. 3 min. From C. Fillingham-Coxwell's *Siberian and Other Folk-Tales: Primitive Literature of the Empire of the Tzars* (1925).

The Crystal Heart

The sheltered and privileged daughter of a mandarin comes to understand the consequences of her naïve yet cruel words to a fisherman when she discovers that he was the singer of the wonderful melody that had captured her heart.

Shepard, Aaron, reteller. 1998. *The Crystal Heart: A Vietnamese Legend.* Illustrated by Joseph Daniel Fiedler. New York: Atheneum. 6 min. This retelling is based on several versions of the tale, including Pham Duy Khiem's "Le Cristal D'Amour" (1951) and L. T. Bach-Lan's " Truong-Chi and Mi-Nuong."

Don't Ever Look at a Mermaid

One day Lutey, a fisherman, encounters a mermaid who asks for his help. Although Lutey had always heard that mermaids were unlucky and that one should never look at one, he could not resist her plea. For his aid, she grants him three wishes but still would have taken his life for looking at her if it weren't for his dog, who breaks the mermaid's spell. Although Lutey's wishes do come true, the mermaid returns to claim him nine years later, and, after that, she claims one of his descendents every nine years. A story of warning from Cornwall.

Mayo, Margaret, reteller. 1996. *Mythical Birds and Beasts from Many Lands*. New York: Dutton, pp. 22–31. 11 min.

Elephant and Hare

The hare plays a series of tricks on an elephant and her fellow hares in order to gorge on a feast of honey.

Ragan, Kathleen, ed. 1998. *Fearless Girls, Wise Women, and Beloved Sisters: Heroines in Folktales from Around the World*. New York: W. W. Norton, pp. 352–353. 4 min. From Naomi Kipury's *Oral Literature of the Maasai* (Heinemann, 1983, 72–74).

A Frog's Gift

To save a frog from a predatory snake, a farmer impulsively promises one of his daughters to be the snake's bride. The youngest daughter travels to her new home with one thousand gourds and one thousand needles and only asks that the groom and his men first sink the gourds and float the needles. While they are attempting this impossible task, she escapes to the home of an old woman. With the woman's help, the heroine finds a much more suitable spouse. As for the old woman, well, she looked a little green!

Martin, Rafe, reteller. 1996. *Mysterious Tales of Japan*. New York: G. P. Putnam's Sons, pp. 52–56. 6 min. This Japanese tale has many Western elements that have developed over the years in the author's retelling of the tale (73).

How the King Chose a Daughter-in-Law

A young peasant girl uses her wits and her spindle of yarn to find the way out of a labyrinth and into marriage with a prince.

Ragan, Kathleen, ed. 1998. *Fearless Girls, Wise Women, and Beloved Sisters: Heroines in Folktales from Around the World*. New York: W. W. Norton, pp. 73–74. 5 min. From Jean Ure's *Rumanian Folk Tales* (Franklin Watts, 1960, 19–21.)

Jackal and Hen

The jackal's plan to capture a hen through a story backfires on him when she is skeptical of the source. The jackal is caught instead!

Ragan, Kathleen, ed. 1998. *Fearless Girls, Wise Women, and Beloved Sisters: Heroines in Folktales from Around the World*. New York: W. W. Norton, pp. 366–67. 4 min. From Minnie Potsma's *Tales from the Bosotho* (University of Texas Press, 1974, 124–31).

Kit Cat of Cat Key

The tall tale adventures of the pirate Calico Jack Rackham and the ship's calico cat Kit Cat when, as a young cabin boy, he is rescued by a dolphin, a mermaid, and a talking cat.

Hausman, Gerald, and Loretta Hausman. 2000. *Cats of Myth: Tales from Around the World*. New York: Simon & Schuster, pp. 65–72. 7 min. Adapted from *Wonderful Adventures on the Ocean: Being True Descriptions of Battles, Tempests, Shipwrecks and*

Perilous Encounters by Captain Hawser Martingale, aka J. S. Sleeper (Locke and Babier, 1858).

The Letter Trick

When her lover comes to visit, a wife dresses him in her clothes and tells her husband that he is her sister. But when the husband sees the man in the morning, the game is up. The quick-witted wife, knowing her husband cannot read, produces a "letter" stating that all her sisters have been changed into men! He tells her that it is true, since he has seen evidence of the transformation with his own eyes.

Carter, Angela, ed. 1992. *The Second Virago Book of Fairy Tales.* London: Virago Press, pp. 32. 2 min. Collected by Melville J. Herskovits and Frances S. Herskovits in *Suriname Folk-Lore* (1936), p. 351. Carter comments, "Storytelling has an important place in this community. Tales were told to entertain the dead as they lay in state. And there was a taboo against telling stories in daytime, because, if you did so, death would come and sit beside you, and you too would die" (213).

The Lytton Girls Who Were Stolen by Giants

Although giants infest the region, two sisters ignore their father's warning and are carried off by giants. The giants treat the girls with kindness but, after four years, the girls manage to escape and return home, bringing important information about the giants to their people.

Ragan, Kathleen, ed. 1998. *Fearless Girls, Wise Women, and Beloved Sisters: Heroines in Folktales from Around the World.* New York: W. W. Norton, pp. 137–38. 5 min. From Franz Boas's *Folk-tales of Salishan and Sahaptin Tribes, Memoirs of the American Folk-Lore Society* (G. E. Stechert, 1917, 38–39).

The Magic Coin

A shopkeeper is given an oddly shaped coin in return for several clay pipes. She sells the pipes to three beautiful women, whom she alone can see. Prosperity comes to the shop, and the shopkeeper and her husband are never in want. Years later the three women return to the shop, and the shopkeeper returns the coin, which she has never spent.

Ragan, Kathleen, ed. 1998. *Fearless Girls, Wise Women, and Beloved Sisters: Heroines in Folktales from Around the World.* New York: W. W. Norton, pp. 279–81. 4 min. From Exaltacion Mercado-Cinco's *A Compilation and a Study of Selected Fairy Tales of Eastern Leyte* (thesis presented to Divine Word University of Tacloban, 1969, 56–59).

Mary Belle and the Mermaid

The river is Mary Belle's companion whenever things become too difficult at home. One day at the river, a mermaid appears, who takes pity on Mary Belle's plight and escorts Mary Belle into the river for a visit with the mermaid's family. The two repeat the visit several times until Mary Belle tells her family. They accompany her to the river and sing the song Mary Belle has always used to summon the mermaid. When the mermaid appears, Mary Belle's father shoots at her, and the mermaid vanishes, never to be seen again. Later Mary Belle walks into the river, and she, too, is never seen again. A "Cinderella-type" story with a very sad ending.

> Hamilton, Virginia. 1995. *Her Stories: African American Folktales, Fairy Tales and True Tales*. New York: Blue Sky, pp. 33–37. 6 min. Based on a cante-fable from South Carolina collected from storyteller Ada Bryan and published by the American Folk-Lore Society in 1923.

Miss Liza and the King

A king is told to learn a trade and is invited to be an apprentice to a shoemaker. He and the shoemaker's daughter trade insults and taunts until he convinces her to marry him. She becomes the queen, but he never learns how to make shoes!

> Philip, Neil, ed. 1999. *Stockings of Buttermilk: American Folktales*. New York: Clarion, pp. 104–111. 9 min. Adapted from Joel Chandler Harris's *Wally Wonderoon and His Storytelling Machine* (New York: Mclure, Phillips & Co., 1902).

Nana Miriam

When a monstrous hippopotamus threatens the Niger village, Nana Miriam's father attempts in vain to get rid of him. Nana Miriam decides to take matters in her own hands and engages it in several decisive magical battles that "showed all the power of a mere girl!" (16).

> Yolen, Jane, reteller. 2000. *Not One Damsel in Distress: World Folktales for Strong Girls*. San Diego, CA: Harcourt Brace Jovanovich, pp. 11–16. 9 min. Retold from *West African Folktales* (Steven H. Gale, NTC, 1995).

Nonikwe and the Great One, Marimba

When the uncle and caregiver of a blind and crippled girl is challenged as corrupt by her father, Marimba, the Great One, travels in disguise to see if the father's claims are true. The young girl and her uncle prove their worthiness and loyalty and Nonikwe is rewarded with a musical instrument Marimba invents, the mukimbe, made of reeds and particularly suitable for use by blind people and those who are ill.

> Ragan, Kathleen, ed. 1998. *Fearless Girls, Wise Women, and Beloved Sisters: Heroines in Folktales from Around the World*. New York: W. W. Norton, pp. 354–58. 9 min. From V. Credo Mutwa's *Indaba, My Children* (Stanmore Press, 1966, 37–41).

O-sung and Han-um

When five-year-old O-sang gets in trouble, his father punishes him by making him count the number of grains of rice in a chest. With the aid of his friend Han-um, the task is done to his father's satisfaction.

Spagnoli, Cathy, reteller. 1998. *Asian Tales and Tellers*. Little Rock, AR: August House. pp. 55–56. 3 min.

Oskus-ool and Dilgizek

When Oskus-ool is in trouble the fox, Dilgizek comes to his aid. Not only does Dilgizek solve Oskus-ool's immediate problems, but he finds Oskus-ool a wife and fortune as well. A close relative of the Puss 'n Boots story, this is one of a cycle of tales about Oskus-ool (Orphan Boy), the hero in many Tuvan epics and tales,

Van Deusen, Kira. 1996. *Shyaan Am! Tuvan Folk Tales*. Bellingham, WA: Udagan Books, pp. 3–7. 6 min.

Oskus-ool and the Golden Princess

Oskus-ool meets many adventures and adventurers on the way to the Golden Lake to fulfill a promise made to his recently deceased father, but once he reaches the lake, his experiences become stranger then ever. His rescue of a fish nets him a princess for a wife, but the adventures keep coming. This is a story of nonstop action featuring the popular Tuvan hero of tales.

Van Deusen, Kira. 1996. *Shyaan Am! Tuvan Folk Tales*. Bellingham, WA: Udagan Books, pp. 35–44. 12 min.

The Pigeon's Bride

The princess was more interested in her embroidery than she was in suitors until she meets a prince who is under a spell to appear as a pigeon during the day. She breaks her promise of confidentiality to the prince, propelling her on a long journey to find her love again. She eventually finds and rescues him by nontraditional means.

Ragan, Kathleen, ed. 1998. *Fearless Girls, Wise Women, and Beloved Sisters: Heroines in Folktales from Around the World*. New York: W. W. Norton, pp. 63–72. 15 min. From Fillmore Parker's *The Laughing Prince, Jugoslav Folk and Fairy Tales* (Harcourt, Brace and World, 1921, 53–72).

The Plucky Maiden

A young maiden faces the decisions made for her with fortitude and wit and, in the long run, makes the important resolutions for herself.

Ragan, Kathleen, ed. 1998. *Fearless Girls, Wise Women, and Beloved Sisters: Heroines in Folktales from Around the World*. New York: W. W. Norton, pp. 219–21. 6 min. From Im Bang and Yi Ryuk's *Korean Folk Tales, Imps, Ghosts and Fairies* (E. P. Dutton, 1913, 83–89).

Rabbit Dances with the People

Jealous Rabbit steals the mask of an insecure dancer, enabling him to attract and dance with several young women. The women become upset when they discover they've been dancing with a rabbit. When the owner of the mask dons it again, the women will have nothing to do with him. When he takes off the mask, he discovers that the women accept him just as he is.

> Ross, Gayle, reteller. 1994. *How Rabbit Tricked Otter and Other Cherokee Trickster Stories.* New York: HarperCollins, pp. 71–75. 4 min.

The Raja Who Dressed in Black

Driven to learn the secret of men who dress only in black, the raja sets out on a quest. Extraordinary adventures culminated in melancholy, the result of his impatience in collecting a kiss from a beautiful and mysterious queen. In the end, the raja discovers the answer to the enigma. He returns home from this unexplained long absence, but now the once hospitable and colorful raja refuses company and dresses only in black. This is one of the seven stories retold from the Persian poem "Haft Paykar," created by the medieval poet Nizami in 1197 as "an allegory for spiritual and moral growth based on the real life and exploits of the Sassanian ruler Shah Bahram V" (from the introduction).

> Tarnowska, Wafa, reteller. 2000. *The Seven Wise Princesses: A Medieval Epic.* New York: Barefoot Books, pp. 15–23. 14 min.

The Silent Witness

A poor man warns a rich man that his horse has a very bad temper and will kill the rich man's horse if they are left next to each other. The poor man's presumptuous advice angers the rich man, who disregards the advice but grows incensed when his horse is indeed killed. When taken before the judge, the poor man refuses to say a word. When the judge observes that the poor man cannot speak, the rich man rushes to explain that the man can in fact speak and repeats the warning the poor man had given him. In so doing, he wins the case for the poor man.

> Hamilton, Martha, and Mitch Weiss, retellers. 2001. *Through the Grapevine: World Tales Kids Can Read and Tell.* Little Rock, AR: August House, pp. 79–81. 4 min. From W. A. Clouston's *Flowers from a Persian Garden* (1890) and Catherine T. Bryce's *Fables from Afar* (1910).

Son of an Otter, Son of a Wolf

King Cormac's youngest daughter becomes pregnant by an otter, and after the baby, a son named Lorcan is born, Lorcan becomes Cormac's pride and joy until Lorcan insists that he is immediately crowned king. He recruits Fionn Cumhail to fight Cormac for the crown. Before the battle, Cormac's new wife begets a son. Cormac leaves the child a belt inscribed "Aidan, son of Cormac." Cormac is killed in battle, and Lorcan becomes an unpopular and unwise king. Cormac's newborn son is taken by a she-wolf moments after his birth and is raised by an old couple. When he matures, he goes to claim his inheritance and, taking the place of his maternal grandfather, is summoned to tell stories all night to King Lorcan. Each night after the sessions of storytelling Aidan taunts Lorcan about his heritage until Lorcan finally discovers that he is indeed the son of an otter and is returned to the sea. Aidan, raised by a wolf, becomes the rightful king of all Ireland.

Doyle, Malachy, reteller. 2000. *Tales from Old Ireland*. New York: Barefoot Books, pp. 52–67. 15 min. Adapted from "The King Who Could Not Sleep" in *Folktales of Ireland* by Sean Sullivan (University of Chicago Press, 1966).

The Soul Cages

Jack lives a comfortable life as a fisherman and scrounger but wishes to meet a Merrow, a man of the sea. Jack's wish comes true when he meets a Merrow, a friend of Jack's own grandfather, and visits him under the sea. Jack is shown the Soul Cages of drowned sailors and hatches a plan to rescue the captured souls. He invites the Merrow to dine with him, gets him drunk, and frees the souls. The Merrow never discovers that the soul cages are empty, and the two remain fast friends. After every severe storm, Jack continues to empty the soul cages.

Doyle, Malachy, reteller. 2000. *Tales from Old Ireland*. New York: Barefoot Books, pp. 68–83. 16 min.

Street Magic

Although this story is presented in comic-book format, it is based on an old Jewish folktale. Eisner's illustrations are so emotional and evocative that the story is especially easy to learn. Cousin Mersh teaches his young cousin how to survive on the streets of New York City in the early part of the twentieth century. Understanding bullies and being quick witted are the two basic tools every New Yorker needs.

Eisner, Will. 2000. *Minor Miracles*. New York: DC Comics, pp. 19–26. 4 min.

Susanna and Simon

Susanna has many suitors, but her father does not approve of any and sets each to impossible tasks. Simon truly loves Susanna and is willing to attempt the tasks set by her witch of a father. Fortunately for the two lovers, Susanna has learned a lot about enchantments from her father.

San Souci, Robert D. 1993. *Cut from the Same Cloth: American Women of Myth, Legend and Tall Tale*. New York: Philomel, pp. 43–48. 6.5 min. Originally included in *Daddy Jake, the Runaway: And Short Stories Told after Dark* by Joel Chandler Harris.

Ti-Jean and the Calf

Ti-Jean and his wife were very poor, but with the aid of a wooden calf, a calfskin, and lucky circumstances, they not only better their circumstances but also defeat their enemies.

Andrews, Jan, reteller. 2000. *Out of the Everywhere: Tales for a New World*. Toronto: Groundwood, pp. 65–72. 8 min. This is a retelling of the Grimms' "The Little Peasant," set in Canada.

The Two Sisters

A prose version of an old ballad, this tale tells of two sisters who compete for the love of one man. The eldest sister murders her rival, but a musician attends her wedding with a strange harp that is strung with the hair of a drowned young woman. The harp sings of the sister's murderous deed and is silent ever more. This version is much kinder to the fiancée, Sir William, than others I have read.

McNeil, Heather. 2001. *The Celtic Breeze: Stories of the Otherworld from Scotland, Ireland and Wales*. Englewood, CO: Libraries Unlimited, pp. 133–39. 8 min. Several ballads that tell the same tale follow the story.

The Unwanted Child

When his child is born, the king is horrified to discover that the baby is repulsive. He turns the baby boy out into the forest, where monkeys take him in and raise him. Years later, the young man witnesses the sacrifice of a beautiful maiden to a serpent, performed to end a drought. He vows to kill the monster and spends the next seven years preparing for battle. Eventually he defeats the serpent and is rewarded by becoming heir to the throne of the rescued princess. Meanwhile, his father is in need of aid and calls on his son for help. At first the unwanted child resists his father's pleas but eventually reconciles and rescues him.

Mama, Raouf, translator and reteller. 1998. *Why Goats Smell Bad and Other Stories from Benin*. North Haven, CT: Linnet, pp. 3–9. 7 min. "The Fon place a high premium on physical beauty, but they place an even higher premium on moral beauty" (9). The author modified the traditional ending of this tale to allow for repentance and reconciliation.

The Wizard Who Got Sick

An Armenian tale about a benevolent wizard who rewards those who show him kindness during his travels. After a year, he retraces his steps to see how the recipients of his gifts are faring. One by one, they refuse to offer him hospitality, so he takes back his gifts until he returns to the home of his first hosts, who welcome him warmly. After that, whenever he feels in poor spirits, he visits the couple, who ease his cares with their compassion.

Matthews, John, and Caitlin Matthews. 1998. *The Wizard King and Other Spellbinding Tales*. New York: Barefoot Books, pp. 56–61. 7 min.

References

de Wit, Dorothy. 1979. *Children's Faces Looking Up: Program Building for the Storyteller*. Chicago: American Library Association.

Livo, Norma J., and Sandra A. Rietz. 1986. *Storytelling: Process and Practice*. Littleton, CO: Libraries Unlimited.

Moran, Barbara. 1987. "The Passive Princess Theme in Traditional Stories." *National Storytelling Journal* 4(3): 21–23.

Phelps, Ethel Johnson, ed. 1978. *Tatterhood and Other Tales*. New York: Feminist Press.

Ragan, Kathleen. 1998. *Fearless Girls, Wise Women and Beloved Sisters*. New York: W. W. Norton.

Ragan, Kathleen. An Interview with Kathleen Ragan. Accessed January 23, 2002, from http://bat.phys.unsw.edu.au/~charley/interview2.html

Shannon, George. 1981. "The Survival of the Child." *Children's Literature in Education*. 12, no. 1: 34–38.

Stein, Mary Beth. 2000. "Folklore and Fairy Tales." In *The Oxford Companion to Fairy Tales*. Edited by Jack Zipes. Oxford: Oxford University Press, 165–170.

Storr, Catherine. 1986. "Folk and Fairy Tales." *Children's Literature in Education*. 17, no. 1:63–70.

Zipes, Jack. 1979. *Breaking the Magic Spell: Radical Theories of Folk and Fairy Tales*. London: Heinemann.

Zipes, Jack. 1983. *Fairy Tales and the Art of Subversion: The Classical Genre for Children and the Process of Civilization*. New York: Wildman Press.

Chapter 5

Tales of Life

One describes a tale best by telling the tale, you see?
The way one describes a story, to oneself or to the
world, is by telling the story. It is a balancing act
and it is a dream. The more accurate the map, the more it
resembles the territory. The most accurate map possible
would be the territory, and thus would be perfectly accurate and perfectly useless. The tale is the map that is the
territory. You must remember this.

—Neil Gaiman, *American Gods*

One of the questions I am often asked when telling stories to young adults is
whether the story is actually true. This seems to be an important point not only
for young adults but for their younger siblings as well. The folktales, I reply, are
not factually true, but they are true in spirit. "Tell us some true stories," they ask.

The suggested stories in this section focus on personalities rather than on
events and can be told just for interest's sake, but they also can be easily incorpo-
rated in the overall school curriculum. Although several of them belong to the
realm of folklore, the majority of the tales are from biographies of people who
have relevance to today's young adults and to their search for identity and personal meaning.

Stories of Romance

One of the key concepts of adolescence discussed by Konopka is the emergence of sexual maturity (Konopka 1973, 299). She claims that sexual maturity generates in young adults "a great wonderment about themselves and the feeling of having something in common with all human beings" (299). It also stimulates young adults to newly assess the world.

Young adults are intensely interested in romantic relationships and the achievement of sexual experience. They enjoy hearing tales that explore the questions and problems that they are also exploring. Nilsen and Donelson, in *Literature for Today's Young Adults,* claim that one of the first types of stories told were romances, because people liked to hear happy endings and enjoyed the exaggeration of the storytellers that made the stories more interesting than real life (1985, 112). In the text, they briefly explore the reasons that romance appeals to young adults. Romance literature, usually concerned with love and adventure, expresses in several ways the preoccupations of young adults:

1. Symbols used in the romance stories often relate to youthfulness and hope, with many of the protagonists being young adults themselves.

2. Young adults, in the middle and late stages of adolescence, are at a point in their lives when they are either leaving home or contemplating leaving. They are embarking on a romantic quest.

3. Large proportions of young adults expend a great deal of time and energy "seeking and securing a 'true love' " and respond to stories that explore romantic relationships.

4. The intensity of emotions honestly felt by young adults is mirrored by the exaggeration that is part of the romantic mode. (Nilsen and Donelson 1985, 113)

Folklore, ancient and modern, is full of references to romance and sexual activity. The love stories in ancient folklore tend to be stark; only the simplest and most artless reasons are offered for love or passion (Yolen, 67). Contemporary legends, the folklore of modern youth, are thinly cloaked sexual cautionary tales. In the literary tales, however, the reasons for love and passion and their consequences are usually explored in greater detail. When telling stories to young adults, remember that they are uncomfortable with risqué humor from a storyteller (if not from their peers) but do appreciate romantic stories that allude to sexuality in a subtle manner.

Family and Local Histories

Stories from local and family histories are also important resources for stories about real life experiences. Young adults can research and develop tales from their own family or community to tell to each other to further develop roots to that family or community.

I often begin storytelling workshops by focusing on the stories behind the personal names of the people in the workshop or classes. We look at three aspects of our names. I first ask the students to discover where their names came from, to ask their families questions about who named them, why their particular names were chosen, and whether the names have a family significance. Second, we turn to books on names and find out what their names might mean. I must admit that this can be aggravating for children who do not have traditional names, but it still makes the point that most words or names have stories beyond their surface meanings. I then ask whether the students like their names. Often this is the first time many of the young adults have given any thought to the story behind their names, and it opens up many other possibilities for story sources.

I recommend that the stories behind the names of towns, streets, schools and other public buildings also be explored. These are often local names that have been taken for granted, but the research unearths a valuable resource for classroom discussions and a sense of pride.

Family conflict can also be sources of story material. Several years ago I watched in great fear as my daughter Taryn was repeatedly thrown off a horse as she attempted to guide it over a jump in a local competition. Taryn was determined that the horse would take the jump; I, on the other hand, was terrified that my daughter would be hurt. My fear of horses is in proportion to the love my daughter has for them. Several weeks after the incident, I was asked to tell a story on the radio. I still had not worked out the fear and frustration I had felt watching Taryn and the horse and decided to do so by having her help me develop a story out of the experience. The story was well received, but it accomplished much more than pleasing my audience. It helped me handle the fears that I have when my daughter goes riding today. I have included a version of this tale, "Taryn's Jump," in Chapter 9, "Sample Stories."

Annotated Bibliography

Andrew's Wolf Pups
When Andrew, a Chipewyan Indian, attempted to use wolf pups as sled dogs in the Canadian north, he found that regardless of how much care and attention he gave them, freedom was what they needed most of all.

Fumoleau, Rene. 1994. In *Next Teller: A Book of Canadian Storytelling*. Collected by Dan Yashinsky. Charlottetown, P.E.I.: Ragweed, pp. 235–40. 6 min.

Ann Maria Weems: "My Child, Is It Really You?"

Ann Marie, at fifteen, was one of the youngest slaves to flee without a parent as a guide to freedom. With some help, she disguised herself as a young carriage driver named Joe Wright and made her way to freedom in Canada in this guise. She made her way to her aunt and uncle who never expected her to see her again.

Fradin, Dennis Brindell. 2000. *Bound for the North Star: True Stories of Fugitive Slaves*. New York: Clarion, pp. 147–54. 11 min.

The Bird Lovers

A pair of lovers continually attempt to be together through many reincarnations, but fate and impatience keep them apart. Finally, as a pair of birds they manage to have some fine years together until fate intercedes once again. A lifetime later, the young man uses the musical instrument, the xim xaus, to win back the love he thought he had lost.

Jaffe, Nina, and Steve Zeitlin, retellers. 1998. *The Cow of No Color: Riddle Stories and Justice Tales from Around the World*. New York: Henry Holt, pp. 59–69. 9 min. The "xim xaus" is made from a coconut, horsehair, and bamboo and is known as a talking instrument because certain sounds stand for certain words, and a person can tell a story by simply bowing the strings. It is known as a courting instrument among the Hmong people of Laos. Also found in Livo, Norma J., and Dia Cha. 1991. *Folk Stories of the Hmong: Peoples of Laos, Thailand, and Vietnam*. Englewood, CO: Libraries Unlimited.

The Black Prince

A young boy traded his flute for his soul to win the girl he loves. He eventually wins her but realizes that she was in love with the young boy he once was and can never be again. A poignant and powerful tale that includes a personal experience of the storyteller as a frame. She gives permission to tell her anecdote as an opening and closing as long as she is credited.

Simms, Laura, reteller. 1994. In *Ready-to-Tell Tales: Sure-Fire Stories from America's Favorite Storytellers*, edited by David Holt and Bill Mooney. Little Rock, AR: August House, pp. 95–99. 5 min.

Boss of the Plains

This is the story of John Stetson and how he came to create the most popular hat west of the Mississippi. While young adults may not be drawn to the picture-book format for this tale, it has a distinct oral quality that makes it suitable for telling to them.

Carlson, Laurie. 1998. *Boss of the Plains: The Hat That Won the West*. Illustrations by Holly Meade. New York: DK Ink. 6 min.

Cape Sable Cats

The author states that this is a family tale about a homesteader in Florida who sought a solution to the rat problem created by the major crop of sugar cane. The plan was not entirely practical, but the rats did disappear!

Congdon, Kristin G. 2001. *Uncle Monday and Other Florida Tales*. Illustrated by Kitty Kitson Petterson. Jackson, MS: University of Mississippi, pp. 33–35. 4 min. From Florida Writers' Project, Department of State, Division of Historical Resources, Florida Folklife Archives.

The Chicken-Coop Jail

Nathan Jackson was a Tory, and because of his loyalty to England and her queen, he went peacefully to jail when the Revolution was over. The jail was a old converted chicken coop; and because Nathan was bored, he renovated the building and made it stronger (as well as more secure). He also made arrangements to work his former land, returning to the jail each evening after a day's work. When the sheriff could not accompany him, Nathan walked fifty-five miles to the county seat to stand trial. On the way, he stopped to give assistance to a man whose carriage wheel had collapsed. He told the man his story, and the man gave him a ride into the town, sparing Nathan the last few miles of his journey. Nathan stood trial and was found guilty, but a governor's pardon, brought to him by the man he had helped, set him free.

De Spain, Pleasant. 2000. *Sweet Land of Story: Thirty-Six American Tales to Tell*. Little Rock, AR: August House, pp. 17–21. 9 min. Told to the author by Harold Johnson, a native of the area.

Coonlagh and the Fairy Maiden

Although his father tried everything he could think of to keep Coonlagh from following his fairy maiden love, it was to no avail. Coonlagh's love was so great that he turned his back on his family and country and followed her to the mystical Land of the Ever Young, Tier Na n'Og.

Husain, Shahrukh, ed. 1993. *The Virago Book of Witches*. London: Virago, pp. 17–19. 6 min. This story has been transcribed from storyteller Pat Ryan's audiotape, *Tales of Old, British and Irish Fairytales* (1985) by the editor. She states that it is probably a nineteenth-century tale and that a literary version appeared in 1925 in Lady Wilde's collection, *Ancient Legends, Mystic Charms and Superstitions of Ireland*. There are similarities to Keats's *La Belle Dame Sans Merci*. The apple, Husain comments, has ancient Celtic associations with the Silver Bough of the Underworld (225).

Fed: "Bound for the North Star"

Fed, or John Brown as he was known as later, started life as a slave on a Virginia plantation. His story recounts his experiences as he was taken from his family and sold to various slave owners and then finally escapes to freedom. He had always dreamed of going to England, and in 1850 he realized his dream.

Fradin, Dennis Brindell. 2000. *Bound for the North Star: True Stories of Fugitive Slaves.* New York: Clarion, pp. 12–31. 20 min.

Georgia O'Keeffe (Skulls and Flowers)

This story, basically a brief sketch of the artist's marriage, fears, desires, and accomplishments, would be useful to introduce students to her work and to a portrait of a strong individual who was secure in her identity and life choices.

Krull, Kathleen. 1995. *Lives of the Artists: Masterpieces, Messes (and What the Neighbors Thought).* San Diego, CA: Harcourt Brace, pp. 69–71. 4 min.

Grimaldi

Grimaldi, the world-famous clown, seeks medical advice incognito from a famous Viennese doctor who could heal the sickness of the soul. The advice is to laugh, in fact, to attend the circus performance of the clown Grimaldi! When informed by his patient of his identity, the doctor could only prescribe a public and violent death. When he attempts to follow the doctor's advice, he finds that the doctor's reputation is well deserved.

Orlandis-Habsburgo, Carmen. 1994. In *Next Teller: A Book of Canadian Storytelling.* Collected by Dan Yashinsky. Charlottetown, P.E.I.: Ragweed, pp. 228–31. 5 min.

Hildegard of Bingen

The life and times of the visionary German nun is brought to life in this condensed look at her life, accomplishments, and music.

Krull, Kathleen. 1999. *They Saw the Future: Oracles, Psychics, Scientists, Great Thinkers, and Pretty Good Guessers.* New York: Atheneum, pp. 35–41. 11 min.

Honeyboy's Gift

Honeyboy's mother is proud of her son even though he is known as a thief and scoundrel with a price on his head. After all, he never neglects her or people in need. When the sheriff fetches her to identify a faceless body that has been killed for the reward, Honeyboy's mother strongly and silently accuses the murderer. While she refuses to give the body a name, she does bring justice for her son. A strong, subtle story.

Torrence, Jackie. 1998. *Jackie Tales: The Magic of Creating Stories and the Art of Telling Them.* New York: Avon, pp. 217–26. 11 min. The author says, "Yes, even crime was different in the thirties. Honeyboy robbed and stole, but he left money and food on people's porches. It was crime, but it was help that people needed too. Honeyboy is both bad and generous, which makes what happens to him interesting" (220).

How the Cheyenne Got Horses

The Spanish conquistadors brought horses to the New World, and when the horses and riders were first sighted by the Cheyenne, they were thought to be monsters. Fear quickly turned to exaltation as the Cheyenne learned to work with horses as well.

Mendoza, Patrick M., Ann Strange Owl-Raben, and Nico Strange Owl. 1998. *Four Great Rivers to Cross: Cheyenne History, Culture and Traditions.* Englewood, CO: Teachers' Idea Press, pp. 37–39. 5 min.

Johnny Draw the Knife

When caught in a storm while fishing, Johnny saves the entire crew of a fishing boat by throwing his knife into the center of a wave. A woman appears at the back of the wave, his knife firmly lodged in her chest. When she cries for Johnny to withdraw his knife, he refuses, and the boat travels safely to shore. As punishment for his actions, Johnny never returns to the sea or to fishing.

Husain, Shahrukh, ed. 1993. *The Virago Book of Witches.* London: Virago, pp. 134–35. 4 min. From *Seal Stories and Belief on Rathlin Island.* Linda-May Ballard and Thomas Cecil, storytellers. *Ulster Folklife* (1983) 29: 40.

Johnny Weissmuller (Looking Good without Clothes)

The story of the record-breaking American swimmer Johnny Weissmuller, winner of five gold medals in the 1924 and 1928 Olympics who became famous as Tarzan in nineteen movies. "With the powerful lungs he'd developed from swimming, Weissmuller came up with Tarzan's famous chest-thumping roar in homage to the yodeling contests at Austrian-German picnics he'd attended as a child" (31).

Krull, Kathleen. 1997. *Lives of the Athletes: Thrills, Spills (and What the Neighbors Thought).* San Diego, CA: Harcourt Brace, pp. 29–31. 4 min.

The Jury

A defense lawyer is attempting to win an acquittal for his client, accused of murdering his missing wife. The lawyer announces to the jury that the women is still alive and walking through the courtroom door as he speaks. His contention is that, because all members of the jury turn to look, there is reasonable doubt in their minds. The jury takes no time in returning with a guilty plea in this case. Why? They noticed that one person did not turn to look at the door expecting to see the wife alive!

Jaffe, Nina, and Steve Zeitlin, retellers. 1998. *The Cow of No Color: Riddle Stories and Justice Tales from Around the World.* New York: Henry Holt, pp. 47–51. 3 min. This story is part truth and part fiction and told by the informant, Justice Eugene Pincham, to demonstrate how astute the members of this jury were (49).

Lookin' Jake

This story tells of the novel's main character Garnet's thoughts and revelations as he spends several days by himself on a canoe trip to a deserted camp. "If you ever wanna get the idea of how it feels to fly, all you really gotta do is paddle a canoe alone across a northern lake when it's calm" (159).

> Wagamese, Richard. 1994. *Keeper'n Me*. Toronto: Doubleday Canada, pp.159–62. 7 min. This is an excerpt from the novel.

Mark Twain (Killingly Funny)

Mark Twain's boyhood and early development as a writer are explored in this brief look at his life and storytelling prowess.

> Krull, Kathleen. 1994. *Lives of the Writers: Comedies, Tragedies (and What the Neighbors Thought)*. San Diego, CA: Harcourt Brace, pp. 57–61. 6 min.

Marshall McLuhan

McLuhan, originator of expressions such as "the global village" and "the medium is the message," made legendary predictions about the technological future, which are featured in this brief exploration of his life and theories. McLuhan considered himself a messenger bearing information about the future, and he didn't want to be criticized because he was the bearer of bad news. " 'The truth shall make you free' was a Bible quote that he liked—and he had it inscribed on his gravestone" (105).

> Krull, Kathleen. 1999. *They Saw the Future: Oracles, Psychics, Scientists, Great Thinkers, and Pretty Good Guessers*. New York: Atheneum, pp. 99–105. 12 min.

Miguel de Cervantes (One Disaster after Another)

The unfortunate pattern of disasters that made up the life of the author of *Don Quixote* is the focus of this brief look at the life of the "father of the modern novel."

> Krull, Kathleen. 1994. *Lives of the Writers: Comedies, Tragedies (and What the Neighbors Thought)*. San Diego, CA: Harcourt Brace, pp. 15–17. 4 min.

Nicholas Black Elk

Nicholas was only nine years old when he had an overwhelming vision relating to the future of the Lakota people. For many years he told no one about it, but his experiences traveling with Buffalo Bill in Europe led to his return to the traditional Lakota way of life. He became a respected medicine man and then, after converting to Christianity, an active missionary. He finally related his vision at age sixty-nine to John Neihardt, who published his words as *Black Elk Speaks* in 1932. The book became popular in the 1970s and continues to influence contemporary Indian activists.

Krull, Kathleen. 1999. *They Saw the Future: Oracles, Psychics, Scientists, Great Thinkers, and Pretty Good Guessers*. New York: Atheneum, pp. 67–73. 11 min.

Peter Ilich Tchaikovsky (Pulsing and Quivering)

Tchaikovsky's strange life of unhappiness and despair was only alleviated by writing music. "He was terrified of literally losing his head while conducting. So he would hold on to it with his left hand while beating time with his right" (56).

Krull, Kathleen. 1993. *Lives of the Musicians: Good Times, Bad Times (and What the Neighbors Thought)*. San Diego, CA: Harcourt Brace, pp. 55–57. 4 min.

The Preacher and the Ducks

When the young girl nibbles on the roast duck she is helping to prepare for the Sunday dinner, she panics about being caught. She invents a story to cover her actions, much to the discomfort of the preacher who arrives to partake of the meal. Her family is not amused when they discover the truth, but the story remains part of the family lexicon of tales.

Congdon, Kristin G. 2001. *Uncle Monday and Other Florida Tales*. Illustrated by Kitty Kitson Petterson. Jackson, MS: University of Mississippi, pp. 103–106. 6 min.

The Proud Horseman

When the proud horseman was approached for a ride by a tired peasant loaded down with food and water, he quickly told him no. But after riding on, he realized that he had forgotten to supply himself with adequate food and water. He returned to help the peasant only to find that he had eaten and drank his fill and rested enough to walk on with out the horseman's help. Now the proud horseman had lost not only time and energy, but a chance to partake of food and water as well.

DeSpain, Pleasant. 1999. *The Emerald Lizard: Fifteen Latin American Tales to Tell in English and Spanish*. Little Rock, AR: August House, pp. 97–99. 3 min. The author states that his version was told to him, but another version can be found in Harold Courlander's *Ride with the Sun: An Anthology of Folk Tales and Stories from the United Nations* (1955).

Pulling the Rope

Lucy and Samuel eloped because Lucy's father did not think Samuel good enough for his daughter. The newlyweds decided to have a contest of strength to see who would make the rules in their new home. They threw a rope over the barn, and then each of them held one end. The first one to pull the rope over the barn would be the boss. But, as Samuel demonstrated, both of them could be winners!

De Spain, Pleasant. 2000. *Sweet Land of Story: Thirty-Six American Tales to Tell*. Little Rock, AR: August House, pp. 37–39. 5 min. Told to the author by Harold Johnson.

Shake Rag

Although it is published as a picture book, this is a very oral story about a period in the childhood of Elvis Presley when he and his family were extremely poor and lived in Shake Rag. It was there that he was introduced to the soulful music of the Sanctified Church that traveled to his town.

Littlesugar, Amy. 1998. *Shake Rag: From the Life of Elvis Presley.* Illustrated by Floyd Cooper. New York: Philomel. 11 min. Includes bibliographical references.

Silver Heels (Colorado)

Silver Heels Jenny, a dance-hall girl in Fairplay, Colorado, fell in love with a young miner. When smallpox arrived in Fairplay and the neighboring community of Buckskin Joe, Silver Heels Jenny's lover perished. She nursed everyone that she could, but after the epidemic was under control, she was nowhere to be found. To show their appreciation, the miners gave her name to the most beautiful mountain in the district, Mount Silver Heels.

Livo, Norma J. 2001. *Story Medicine: Multicultural Tales of Healing and Transformation.* Englewood, CO: Libraries Unlimited, pp. 158–59. 4 min

The Visit

Hospitality is an essential element of Indian values, and it is demonstrated in this brief true tale about a couple who are given food, shelter and kindness from strangers.

Spagnoli, Cathy. 1998. *Asian Tales and Tellers.* Little Rock, AR: August House, pp. 86–87. 2 min. A true anecdote told to the author by Professor Rastogi in Delhi, India.

Where the Girl Rescued Her Brother

The true story of Buffalo Calf Road Woman's heroic rescue of her brother during the Battle of the Rosebud. Both sides of the conflict stopped fighting to watch her ride into battle, help her brother onto the back of her horse, and then carry him to safety. Background information about the courage of Cheyenne women is also part of the story.

Bruchac, Joseph, and Gayle Ross, retellers. 1994. *The Girl Who Married the Moon: Tales from Native North America.* New York: Bridgewater, pp. 101–107. 13 min.

Wine as Doctor

Wine in the district of Bernkastel, Germany, was known as Doctor for more than five hundred years when a soldier cured an ailing Bishop with the fiery regional wine.

Livo, Norma J. 2001. *Story Medicine: Multicultural Tales of Healing and Transformation.* Englewood, CO: Libraries Unlimited, pp. 15–16. 3 min.

Woody Guthrie (Traveling Troubadour)
The legendary Woody Guthrie and his love of music and words is the focus of this tale about a traveling man who left his mark on the world of American folk music, ballads, and children's songs.

Krull, Kathleen. 1993. *Lives of the Musicians: Good Times, Bad Times (and What the Neighbors Thought)*. San Diego, CA: Harcourt Brace, pp. 91–93. 4 min.

Zora Neale Hurston (She Jumped at the Sun)
The outrageous exploits of this famous African American novelist and reteller of folktales forms the backbone of this story.

Krull, Kathleen. 1994. *Lives of the Writers: Comedies, Tragedies (and What the Neighbors Thought)*. San Diego, CA: Harcourt Brace, pp. 83–85. 4 min.

References

Konopka, Gisela. 1973. Requirements for Healthy Development of Adolescent Youth. *Adolescence* 8(3): 21–23.

Nilsen, Alleen Pace, and Kenneth L. Donelson. 1985. *Literature for Today's Young Adults*. 2nd ed. Glenview, IL: Scott, Foresman.

Yolen, Jane. 1986. *Favorite Folktales from around the World*. New York: Pantheon.

Chapter 6

Tales of the Spirit

---

*H*omer, Pindar and other early poets call the satyrs and centaurs *pheres.*. . . This word is applied to things that hunt and are hunted; it means *creatures of the wild*. It is sister to the Latin *ferus*, whose descendants in English include the words *feral, ferocious*, and *fierce*. Faerie is, or was once, not a playground filled with diminutive amusements for young minds but the myth-world itself, which is everything outside of our control. Faerie is an old name for the world of nonhumans that surrounds, feeds and (sometimes) tolerates us all.

—Robert Bringhurst, from the Introduction to
Alice Kane's *The Dreamer Awakes*

More so than when first writing about myths and legends a decade ago, I believe that young adults need a strong background in world mythology in order to better understand and appreciate the world of popular culture that surrounds them. The stories are also extremely powerful and well suited to a young adult audience.

Myths

Myths are attempts to explain cosmic phenomena, natural history, the origins of human civilization, and the origins of religious and social customs (Sutherland 1981, 197). Myths, particularly Greco-Roman myths, are the source of innumerable allusions the listener will encounter again and again in literary, artistic, and even commercial endeavors. "The myths of Psyche and Eros, or Oedipus are so fundamental that their very names have become symbols larger than themselves" (Egoff 1981, 210).

> In myth we see religion, philosophy, art, sociology, anthropology, history, and science coming together to give us a sense of the deepest truths and energies of humankind. That the patterns of myth are paralleled in different cultures, that the same basic story occurs again and again in the basic archetypes of myth, suggests the human need for myth and the connection between myth and language, myth and dream, and myth and human understanding of the mystery of the universe. At the center of each culture's mythologies lies the need to understand the ineffable, to answer the basic and essential questions of why are we here, how did we get here, and what is our purpose in being here? (Leeming 1997, 321)

Native North American myths often resemble the myths of other lands. "Prometheus stole fire for the Greeks; Raven stole it for the West Coast Indians; Nanabozho for the Ojibway or Chippewas; and Glooscap for the East Coast Indians" (Egoff 1975, 20). The native people of North America do not make the distinction between god and hero that is found in other cultures, and for that reason many of their myths are referred to, improperly, as legends (Egoff 1975, 21).

Pourquoi Myths

Pourquoi myths, or origin stories, explain why and how the natural phenomena of the world came into being. The stories include rationalizations for cosmic phenomena such as an explanation of why the sky is separate from earth to the smallest details about the physiology of plant and animal characteristics and habits and artifacts of humankind. These stories are entertaining, but they also include a wealth of information about the natural world because they are based on careful observation. They have multiple functions:

- To pass on knowledge and information

- To teach lessons about danger or the power of nature

- To impart the culture's values and reverence towards the gifts of the earth

- To give environmental warnings

- To present the wildlife and landscape of regions

- To reveal a people who felt themselves to be very much a part of nature (Kraus 1998, 3)

These tales are usually quite short and appeal to young adult tellers as well as listeners. There are numerous Pourquoi tales in this chapter.

Legends

Legends tell the stories of the heroes of old, whereas myths deal chiefly with the gods and forces of nature in the remote past of an earlier world. Legends often contain mythical elements but are based on some historical truth. They frequently tell of the tests that a hero must pass in growing from a powerless child to a position of leadership in society. They appeal to young adults because young adults continually imagine themselves as heroes. They like the excitement, admire the virtues of the heroes, and understand the heroes' human weaknesses. Heroes are vital to every society because they provide people with examples of realistic men and women who, almost incidentally, have magical powers or extraordinary qualities.

Myths, Legends, and the Young Adult

Myths and legends are a necessary part of a reader's education. Northrop Frye (quoted in Stohler 1987) claims that education brings true freedom when it teaches the child to imagine and transform the existing social order. "Such education begins," says Frye, "where literature begins, that is in the teaching of mythology, legends and folktales" (31). Stohler emphasizes that myths and legends are not just entertaining but essential to the emotional growth and development of the imagination of young adults. Young adults, as they mature, begin to take the stories and images as patterns and metaphors that enrich their imaginations and allow them to consider the world in deeper terms (31). What was real or quasi-real for a young child becomes an ideal whose truth is symbolic, rather than literal, for the young adult.

Literature becomes more meaningful and enjoyable when young adults can understand the allusions in the literature by understanding the myths and legends behind them. A vital ingredient in the progression toward becoming a mature reader is traditional mythical stories. They keep alive "an awareness of the primitive associations and worlds that lie behind complex novels" (Alywin 1981, 83).

Myths and legends, although far removed from modern society, deal with universal emotions and dilemmas that young adults are exploring. They are tales of initiation. The initiatory ordeals include battles with monsters, insurmountable obstacles, riddles to be solved, and impossible tasks. The protagonists pass "by way of a symbolic death and resurrections, from ignorance and immaturity to the spiritual age of an adult" (Eliade 1963, 201).

At the same time, one of the most difficult discussions for some students is the one on mythology because of the popular meaning that has become associated with the word "myth." To many it means a falsehood, and the media perpetuates this misunderstanding by publishing articles or airing segments with titles such as "Ten Common Myths about . . ."; the term they should use is misconceptions.

Young adults should be familiar with the myths that have evolved from their own background, but they should also be acquainted with the myths of other cultures. This is one road to human understanding and world peace. But it is more than that. The classic myths of the Greeks and Romans and the more earthy myths of the Norse are reflected daily in our North American culture and language. The days of the week and the names of the months reflect mythic origins, for example. The Romans dedicated the first month of the year to their two-faced god, Janus, because one face could look forward to the New Year, while the other face looked back on the year just completed. More of these word origin stories will be explored in Chapter 8.

Annotated Bibliography

Acrefoot Johnson

Acrefoot was Florida's legendary barefoot mailman. In this tale, he outraces a fresh horse and brand-new buggy driven by a judge.

Congdon, Kristin G. 2001. *Uncle Monday and Other Florida Tales.* Illustrated by Kitty Kitson Petterson. Jackson, MI: University of Mississippi, pp. 72–74. 4 min.

Arrowhead Finger

Gatherer is captured by enemy warriors, who torture her by holding her hands in the fire. Because she does not call out, they call her Arrowhead Finger and leave her be. She heals her fingers with the plants she has gathered. As her hands heal, her enemies return her hands to the fire, and she again heals the wounds. The cycle continues until, afraid her enemies will discover the plant, she swallows it. Eventually the plant becomes a child inside of Arrowhead Finger, and when it is born, the child warns her of danger. She escapes to return to her village. The child becomes a medicine guide for Arrowhead Finger and the people.

Bruchac, Joseph, and Gayle Ross. 1994. *The Girl Who Married the Moon: Tales from Native North America*, pp. 13–20. 8 min.

Bigfoot

This is Roger Patterson's story as he follows Bigfoot and captures the creature on film in 1967. The film is analyzed for details that will reveal it is a hoax, but it proves to be authentic. Bigfoot sightings are still greeted with skepticism, although some jurisdictions in the Pacific Northwest have the Sasquash listed as a legally protected species (85).

Leeming, David, and Jake Page. 1999. *Myths, Legends, and Folktales of America: An Anthology.* New York: Oxford University Press, pp. 81–85. 6 min.

Bow and Arrow

The traditional courtship of Kesedilwe and Kora Kora Due culminates in Kora Kora Due's shooting an arrow at his beloved. If she accepts his marriage proposal, she will calmly remove the arrow from her body; if she rejects him, she will snap the arrow in two.

Lewis, I. Murphy, collector. 1997. *Why Ostriches Don't Fly and Other Tales from the African Bush.* Englewood, CO: Libraries Unlimited, pp. 37–45. 8 min.

The Buffalo Wins!

The conflict between the king of Java and the people of West Sumatra is decided by a battle between a mean, powerful buffalo and a buffalo calf that has yet to be weaned.

Terada, Alice. M. 1994. *The Magic Crocodile and Other Folktales from Indonesia.* Honolulu, HI: University of Hawaii Press, pp. 6–8. 3 min.

The Cast-Off Skin

"Some folk say that in the beginning, people did not die. Rather they cast their skins like snakes and crabs, and thus renewed their youth" (9). One day, when an old woman casts off her skin, her daughter does not recognize her and is completely distraught. The woman returns to find her skin and dons it and, when it was time, she died. Since that time, people no longer cast away their old skins.

Gignoux, Jane Hughes. 1998. *Some Folk Say: Stories of Life, Death, and Beyond.* New York: FoulkeTale Publishing, pp. 9–10. 3 min. Adapted from Dixon, Roland B., *The Mythology of All Races.* Vol. IX, *Oceanic* (Marshall Jones, 1916).

Chipmunk Girl and Owl Woman

Chipmunk Girl loved to pick berries in the woods, and it is in the berry patch that she first encounters Owl Woman, who steals and eats children. They have a battle of wits, and Owl Woman scratches the back of Chipmunk Girl's dress. Since that battle, chipmunks have always had striped backs. During her search to find Chipmunk Girl, Owl Woman causes physical changes to Meadowlark and to herself before she is tricked and defeated by Coyote.

Bruchac, Joseph, and Gayle Ross. 1994. *The Girl Who Married the Moon: Tales from Native North America*, pp. 108–15. 8 min.

The Death of Balder

Balder the Good's death, the result of Loki's trickery, leads to the destruction of the Norse pantheon in Asgard. To escape punishment, Loki flees to the mountains, where he invents the fishing net. He is responsible for the present form of the salmon, the form he was wearing when Thor captured him, and for causing earthquakes when he writhes in horror at his eternal punishment.

Gignoux, Jane Hughes. 1998. *Some Folk Say: Stories of Life, Death, and Beyond.* New York: FoulkeTale Publishing, pp. 68–72. 8 min. Another version can be found in the following text: Steve Zeitlin. 2000. *The Four Corners of the Sky: Creation Stories and Cosmologies from Around the World.* New York: Henry Holt, pp. 55–58.

Dreamcatcher Story

In his wish to be like other children, a crippled boy is told to believe in the power of dreams. To help him, his grandmother makes him a dreamcatcher, and finally, when the boy believes wholeheartedly in the power of dreams, the dreamcatcher brings him good fortune.

Max, Jill. Ed. 1997. *Spider Spins a Story: Fourteen Legends from Native America.* Flagstaff, AZ: Northland, pp. 59–61. 4 min.

Drop Star

The story of a young girl who disappears from her home, devastating her widowed mother. Years later, an oblique message reveals to the mother that her daughter is still alive, and the mother sets off to reclaim her from the chief who snatched her many years before. As mother and daughter, now known as Drop Star, watch in horror, the chief goes on a final journey to find his own daughter, who had died some time before. He smashes a hole in his canoe and vanishes into the lake forever. The lake has been known as "Drop Star" or Kayutah since that time. "Drop Star" appears to be a local tale popularized by the white settlers who moved to upstate New York. This is an interesting example of a place name legend that celebrates the young rescued woman rather than the man who makes the lake his final destination.

San Souci, Robert D., reteller. *Cut from the Same Cloth: American Women of Myth, Legend and Tall Tale.* New York: Philomel, pp. 21–26. 10 min.

The Emerald Lizard

The revered Brother Pedro San Joseph de Bethancourt, known for his kindness and for producing miracles, helps a poor man and his ailing wife. Brother Pedro transforms a lizard into an emerald, which the man then sells, using the money he earns to cure his wife. Years later, the man reclaims the emerald and returns it to Brother Pedro, who turns the emerald back into a lizard.

DeSpain, Pleasant. 1999. *The Emerald Lizard: Fifteen Latin American Tales to Tell in English and Spanish*. Little Rock, AR: August House, pp. 15–17. 3 min.

Finn and the Salmon of Knowledge

The story of Finn MacCoul's conception, birth, and early life and the incident in which he inadvertently tastes the salmon of knowledge. Finn's story is continued in the story titled "Finn MacCoul" summarized in the next entry.

Heaney, Marie. 2000. *The Names upon the Harp: Irish Myth and Legend*. London: Faber and Faber, pp. 62–70. 8 min.

Finn MacCoul

An ancient prophecy states that a person named Finn would be the eater of the salmon of knowledge and thus become a great poet. Finn the Seeker hired a young servant, Demne, to help him catch the salmon and cook it for him. But Demne had other names as well—Finn MacCoul—and it was for him that the prophecy awaited. This concise version of the legend also relates the story of Finn's wife and son. The Finn cycle of stories, translated into English from Old Irish in the late 1700s, tells of Finn and his nomadic warriors, the Fianna, roaming the south of Ireland in the third century.

Osborne, Mary Pope, reteller. 1998. *Favorite Medieval Tales*. New York: Scholastic, pp. 2–7. 7 min.

Five Poppy Seeds

A grieving mother who cannot accept the death of her child is sent to find five poppy seeds from a home that has never experienced death.

Gignoux, Jane Hughes. 1998. *Some Folk Say: Stories of Life, Death, and Beyond*. New York: FoulkeTale Publishing, pp. 142. 1 min. From *The Teachings of Buddha* by Buddhist Promoting Foundation (Kosiado Printing, 1966).

The Girl and the Puma

A young woman who, along with the entire frontier community, faces starvation, disobeys the captain and slips away from the fort to find something to eat. She quickly realizes she is in danger. The enemy, wild animals, and even her own people pose a threat, so she hides in a cave. Inside the cave she finds a distressed puma giving birth to the second of two cubs and quickly gives aid. She stays with the puma family until Querandi Indians capture her and take her to live in their village. But soon men from the fort lay siege to the Indian village and take her back to the fort, where she is sentenced to death for disobeying the captain. In her anger, she replies that the puma and Indians were never as cruel to her as he is. Instead of hanging her, the captain decides to tie her to a tree, left at the mercy of the wild animals. The puma and cubs protect her until the people from the fort rescue her. She is welcomed back into her community and lives a long and courageous life.

> Yolen, Jane, reteller. 2000. *Not One Damsel in Distress: World Folktales for Strong Girls*. San Diego, CA: Harcourt, 27–32. 7 min. A simple version can be found in the following text: DeSpain, Pleasant. 1999. *The Emerald Lizard: Fifteen Latin American Tales to Tell in English and Spanish*. Little Rock, AR: August House, pp. 115–19.

The Girls Who Almost Married an Owl

Two sisters do not want to be separated, even by marriage, and so they look for a fine husband to share. Owl overhears their plan and pretends to be the man the girls seek—an Indian chief. The owl's grandmother takes pity on the kind girls and foils his plan. They return home and marry the men their parents have selected for them and live long and prosperous lives.

> Bruchac, Joseph, and Gayle Ross. 1994. *The Girl Who Married the Moon: Tales from Native North America*, pp. 58–61. 5 min.

God Battles the Queen of the Waters

In a contemporary retelling of Hebrew legend, God battles Tehom, the queen of the waters, when creating the world and imprisons her at the bottom of the sea. God creates sand around the confined bodies of water, which repels the onslaught of the furious water. To this day, the waters are still angry and try to reclaim the world, but the porous sand continues to protect the land.

> Lester, Julius. 1999. *When the Beginning Began: Stories about God, the Creatures, and Us*. San Diego, CA: Silver Whistle, pp. 7–10. 5 min.

The Gossiping Clams

The clams loved to gossip, but their malicious words caused much dissent among their fellow creatures until Beaver buried them in the sand when the tide was out. Since that time, whenever clams open their mouths to gossip, sand and water fill the space. To this day, when walking down a beach, you can still witness clams spitting out water when they try to gossip!

> Baltuck, Naomi, reteller. 1995. *Apples from Heaven: Multicultural Folk Tales about Stories and Storytellers*. North Haven, CT: Linnet, pp. 81–82. 2 min. Adapted from Arthur Griffin's *Ah Mo: Indian Legends from the Northwest* (1990).

The Greedy Father

Beautiful Gbessi's father is poor and greedy. He is holding out for a suitor who will pay a high price for the hand of his daughter. One day a stranger arrives with enough wealth that the greedy father does not hesitate to offer his daughter to him. Although the man looks handsome, he is really a monkey who at first tries to maintain his human ways. He soon tires of working so hard, though, and his wife discovers his identity. Unfortunately she does not escape in time, and her father witnesses her irreversible transformation to match her mate.

> Mama, Raouf, translator and reteller. 1998. *Why Goats Smell Bad and Other Stories from Benin*. North Haven, CT: Linnet, pp. 51–55. 5 min. "He or she who married a stranger may be exposing himself or herself to terrible danger." This story captures the metamorphosis motif in African literature, a motif that goes to the heart of the African colonial experience. Ngugi Wa Thiong'o, the great Kenyan writer, uses a variant of this tale in his short story, "A Meeting in the Dark" (55).

Green Willow

Tomotada, a young samurai, falls in love with a beautiful maiden, Green Willow. They marry and live a life of happiness until someone decides to cut down several willow trees. A story of love and respect for nature that also has spooky undertones.

> Martin, Rafe, reteller. 1996. *Mysterious Tales of Japan*. New York: G. P. Putnam's Sons, pp. 12–16. 6 min. The author explains that the ending has deviated from the one most commonly known through the retellings of Lafcadio Hearn. "I let the growing cycle of death and renewal, appropriate to trees, carry the story further" (71).

How Chameleon Became a Teacher

Chameleon and Crocodile are friends until one day crocodile invites chameleon to his home and attempts to eat him. Chameleon was not quite sure of the invitation, and his timidity and caution save his life. "And so it was that Chameleon became a teacher of prudence and wisdom" (88).

> Mama, Raouf, translator and reteller. 1998. *Why Goats Smell Bad and Other Stories from Benin*. North Haven, CT: Linnet, pp. 87–89. 3 min. "A cautionary tale that warns people against putting their trust in a "friend" without first submitting him or her to a test" (89).

How the Spider Got Its Web

Spider visits Old Man for help catching food. Old Man gives Spider a ball of string but no instructions on how to employ this gift. That, Old Man told him, was something he would have to figure out himself. In disgust and in hunger, Spider swallows the string, but when faced with danger he finds out just what he can do.

> Max, Jill. Ed. 1997. *Spider Spins a Story: Fourteen Legends from Native America*. Flagstaff, AZ: Northland, pp. 17–18. 3 min.

La Escalara Famosa (The Famous Stair)

The story of the building of the staircase in Santa Fe's Loreto Chapel by a mysterious carpenter who arrived as an answer to the nuns' prayers to St. Joseph.

DeSpain, Pleasant. 2000. *Sweet Land of Story: Thirty-Six American Tales to Tell.* Little Rock, AR: August House, pp. 136–39. 5 min.

Lake Phewa

"In the mountainous areas of Nepal, it is difficult to find shelter for the night. This story emphasizes the importance of keeping one's door open to the traveler" (40). When the people of a village deep in the Pokhara Valley deny a *sadhu* (Hindu holy man) shelter, he warns that the dam above the village will break, leaving Lake Phewa to flood the village and threaten its inhabitants. No one believes him, except a simple woman who takes pity on him. In the end, she is the only survivor of the flood. This story explains the origin of the old saying, "The guest is like a visiting god."

Shrestha, Kavita Ram and Sarah Lamstein. 1997. *From the Mango Tree and Other Folktales from Nepal.* Englewood, CO: Libraries Unlimited, pp. 40–43. 7 min. Lake Phewa or Phewatal is the largest and most beautiful of the five lakes in the Pokhara Valley (43).

Lech and the Nest

Duke Lech battles the mother eagle to steal one of her chicks for himself, but as the mother fights more and more gallantly, the Duke becomes increasingly ashamed of his action. To commemorate his realization , Lech created a city, Gniezno (the Eagle's Nest) and a banner, which in time became the Polish flag.

Czarnota, Lorna MacDonald. 2000. *Medieval Tales That Kids Can Read and Tell.* Little Rock, AR: August House, pp. 47–48. 3min. "According to the legends of the founding of Gniezno, which is [one] of Poland's medieval cities, Duke Lech had two brothers, Czech and Rus, who went on to found Czechoslovakia and Russia" (49).

Legend of the Rice Seed

In a tale reminiscent of the Greek myth of Demeter and Persephone, this is the tale of a young daughter of a poor widow who marries the Lord Dragon of the river. Her son-in-law gives the widow some magic rice seeds, instructing her that if there is too much, she is to stand in the field and whistle three times and then clap her hands three times. This advice works for her, and to this day, the people do not whistle or clap while in their rice fields.

Livo, Norma J., and Dia Cha. (1991) *Folk Stories of the Hmong: Peoples of Laos, Thailand, and Vietnam.* Englewood, CO: Libraries Unlimited, pp. 34–35. 2 min.

The Legend of the Windigo

When people begin to vanish from the village, the villagers know a Windigo has moved into the woods. They build a sweat lodge to aid the elders in purifying themselves before tackling the stone monster. A young boy notices that the heat breaks a stone, and this gives him an idea. He tells the elders, who dig a pit and cover it with branches. The Windigo falls through the branches, and the elders and set the pit ablaze. The heat breaks the monster into tiny pieces, each one becoming an insect that haunts people forever: the mosquito!

> Ross, Gayle, reteller. 1996. *The Legend of the Windigo: A Tale from Native North America.* Illustrated by Murv Jacob. New York: Dial. 7 min.

The Little Flying Fox

The little flying fox, an Australian bat, thinks he is a bird and insists that the Great Spirit teach him and other birds, how to be one, in the Dreamtime. The Great Spirit keeps warning the little flying fox to be patient, but eventually, the Great Spirit's patience waned. The flying fox forever hangs upside down as a reminder of that cheeky ancestor.

> McLeod, Pauline E., reteller. 2001. In *Gadi Mirrabooka: Australian Aboriginal Tales from the Dreaming,* edited by Helen F. McKay. Englewood, CO: Libraries Unlimited, pp. 64–65. 3 min. "In this story of the little flying fox, there are sixteen to twenty lessons. It is not the storyteller's responsibility to tell you what they are, but the listener's task to find the lessons hidden within the story" (64).

The Magic Millstones

King Frodi of Iceland is a greedy king who, once gaining the help of two women to grind out gold (and peace and happiness) with the magic millstones, will not let the two women rest. They grind out warriors to stop the king and eventually escape to the sea with the warriors and the millstones. The warriors are also greedy and refuse to let the two women rest. They ask for salt to be ground, and so it was. And so it is to this day!

> Mayo, Margaret. Reteller. 1995. *When the World Was Young: Creation and Pourquoi Tales.* New York: Simon & Schuster, pp. 54–59. 8 min. Based on a myth first published in the *Prose Edda* (1220).

The Mountain Goats of Temlahan

The villagers of Temlahan mistreat the mountain goats until the day village hunters receive a visit from strangers dressed in goatskin blankets and mountain-goat headdresses. Of the hunting party, only a young boy who has been kind to the goats is spared to teach the women, children, and old men left in the village, far below the mountain, how to treat the mountain goats with kindness.

MacDonald, Margaret Read, reteller. 1999. *Earth Care: World Folktales to Talk About*. North Haven, CT: Linnet, pp. 66–70. 7 min. First published in Franz Boas's *The Thirty-First Annual Report of the Bureau of American Ethnology 1909–1910*.

Music for the Tsar of the Sea

A fine retelling of the Russian legend of the musician Sadko and his bargain with the ruler of the underwater realms. After his second visit to the undersea realm, the ruler sends his daughter Volkova to the surface with Sadko to make sure he returns, but during the night she transforms herself. Now the city of Novgorod has a river, the river Volkov.

Lottridge, Celia Barker. 1998. *Music for the Tsar of the Sea*. Illustrations by Harvey Chan. Toronto: Groundwood. 11 min.

Naomi and Ruth

This Biblical tale of Ruth's care and devotion for her mother-in-law is retold with simplicity and grace.

Evetts-Secker, Josephine, reteller. 1996. *Mother and Daughter Tales*. London: Barefoot Books, pp. 74–77. 5 min.

Niall of the Nine Hostages

Niall, High King of Tara, tells of his early experiences as a young man and the challenges he had to face—fire, the kissing of the hag—and of his conviction that he was destined to rule all of Ireland.

McNeil, Heather. 2001. *The Celtic Breeze: Stories of the Otherworld from Scotland, Ireland and Wales*. Englewood, CO: Libraries Unlimited, pp. 40–44. 6 min. The story is followed by a ballad of one of the descendants of Niall, Macneill of Barra.

On a Turtle's Back

This creation story, told by the Six Nations of the Iroquois Confederacy, credits turtle and the crawfish. Crawfish brought mud from the bottom of the ocean and spread it on the turtle's back, where the Sky Woman landed safely after falling from the sky.

Zeitlin, Steve. 2000. *The Four Corners of the Sky: Creation Stories and Cosmologies from Around the World*. New York: Henry Holt, pp. 90–93. 4 min.

The Origin of Puget Sound and the Cascade Range

Ocean gladly sent his sons and daughters, Clouds and Rain, to help the people in time of drought. Soon the people had plenty of water and food but became greedy and refused to allow Clouds and Rain to return to their father. The Great Spirit punished the people by creating the Cascade Mountains and Puget Sound. Ocean still sends very little moisture over the mountains so the people still suffer today.

MacDonald, Margaret Read, reteller. 1999. *Earth Care: World Folktales to Talk About*. North Haven, CT: Linnet, pp. 108–9. 3 min. First published in Ella E. Clark's *Indian Legends of the Pacific Northwest* (University of California Press, 1953).

Orpheus

The tale of the Texas guitar picker Orpheus and his attempted rescue of his beloved wife Eurydice from The Man.

McBride-Smith, Barbara. 1998. *Greek Myths, Western Style: Toga Tales with an Attitude*. Little Rock, AR: August House, pp. 21–25. 7 min.

Osage Spider Story

The clans were choosing a being to guide them and to be their life symbol. The clans sent out runners to search the land for such a being, but one clan was late and ran into a spider during its desperate search. The spider explained why it was the perfect life symbol: everyone comes to it and the home it builds. From that time on, the clan was no longer nomadic and the spider became its life symbol.

Max, Jill. Ed. 1997. *Spider Spins a Story: Fourteen Legends from Native America*. Flagstaff, AZ: Northland, pp. 19–22. 5 min.

Pandora

The story of Pandora and her curiosity is retold with a contemporary flavor. "Just in the nick of time, Pandora got a grip on herself and slammed down the lid and Hope was kept safe in the box" (75).

McBride-Smith, Barbara. 1998. *Greek Myths, Western Style: Toga Tales with an Attitude*. Little Rock, AR: August, pp. 71–75. 5 min.

The Phoenix and Her City

The people of Ningxia work with the Phoenix to transform a wasteland into a place of prosperity, and, because of their mutual respect for each other, the Phoenix comes to live with the people. She goes to battle to protect them when their contentment begins to trouble a greedy official. The city of Yinchaun is called the "Phoenix City" to honor her sacrifice.

Ragan, Kathleen, ed. 1998. *Fearless Girls, Wise Women, and Beloved Sisters: Heroines in Folktales from Around the World*. New York: W. W. Norton, pp. 222–27. 10 min. From Shujiang Li and Karl Luckert's *Mythology and Folklore of the Hui, a Muslim Chinese People* (State University of New York Press, 1994, 132–137).

Rahu's Ragged Throat

This Indian creation tale explains the eclipse of the sun and the moon. Of all the Demons only Rahu will attempt to drink the elixir of immortality that he helped to create. The sun and moon inform Vishnu of this, thus earning them the eternal revenge of the Imp of Eclipses.

> Zeitlin, Steve. 2000. *The Four Corners of the Sky: Creation Stories and Cosmologies from Around the World*. New York: Henry Holt, pp. 46–48. 3 min.

The River

When his kayak overturns, Ebar finds himself in a strange land and, for nine nights, witnesses the water's destruction of the riverbank. On the tenth night, he falls into the river and is trapped by the current. When he cries out for help, it is not his voice that emerges but that of a newborn child. A story of reincarnation from northern Alaska.

> Gignoux, Jane Hughes. 1998. *Some Folk Say: Stories of Life, Death, and Beyond*. New York: FoulkeTale Publishing, pp. 114–15. 3 min. Adapted from Frederica de Laguna's *Under Mount Saint Elias: The History and Culture of the Yakatat Tlingit* (Smithsonian Institute, 1972).

Savitri and Satyavan

Savitri, with the blessing of her father, goes on a journey to find a husband. She falls in love with Satyavan, a young woodcutter, and marries him. Savitri is warned that Satyavan does not have long to live and so prepares herself to gather his soul back from Yamraj, the king of the Underworld. Yamraj not only reunites Savitri with her beloved husband, he also restores Satyavan's inheritance.

> Evetts-Secker, Josephine, reteller. 1997. *Father and Daughter Tales*. Richmond Hill, Ontario: Scholastic Canada, pp. 52–59. 7 min.

Tien-Hou: The Sailor Goddess

This mystical tale from Mei-chou, just off the coast of China, explains how an ordinary girl became the well-respected sailor goddess whose image is a companion on most of the fishing and sailing vessels in China.

> Spencer, Ann. 2001 *Song of the Sea: Myths, Tales, and Folklore*. Toronto: Tundra, pp. 15–19. 5 min.

Ugly Face

A Mohawk monster, Akon:wara' (Ugly Face), is used as a threat to make Blue Sky behave properly. Blue Sky does not believe in the monster's existence, much to his everlasting dismay. A cautionary tale that is still told today.

> Bruchac, Joseph, and James Bruchac. 1998. *When the Chenoo Howls: Native American Tales of Terror*. New York: Walker, pp. 21–27. 7 min.

Uncle Monday

Uncle Monday, an escaped slave and medicine man, had the power to transform into an alligator. This is the story of how he changed himself into an alligator when challenged by a braggart named Judy and of the lesson Judy learned from the experience.

> Congdon, Kristin G. 2001. *Uncle Monday and Other Florida Tales*. Illustrated by Kitty Kitson Petterson. Jackson, MS: University of Mississippi, pp. 55–58. 6 min. From Florida Writers' Project, Department of State, Division of Historical Resources, Florida Folklife Archives.

Vikram and the Dakini

King Vikram's adventures place him in the service of another king, the goddess Kali, and a dakini, the goddess' handmaiden. Thinking that he is unknown to Kali, Vikram requests three wishes from the goddess after he completes his deed. When she grants them, he realizes that not only did she know who he was all along, but she also had engineered his adventure.

> Husain, Shahrukh, ed. 1993. *The Virago Book of Witches*. London: Virago, pp. 177–81. 10 min. Retold by the editor. King Vikram appears to be a composite of several hero kings in Indian folktales. "All storytellers tended to digress occasionally, particularly when dealing with well-known characters such as Vikram or Kali who have a cumulative fairytale tradition, apart from being part of mythology/history" (240).

Why the Sky Is Separate from the Earth

When the world was finished, the sky was not separate from the earth and acted, in fact, like a too-low ceiling. One woman became so frustrated when cooking with a long stick that kept hitting the sky, she used the stick as a spear and broke the sky into tiny little clouds and a high ceiling.

> Sherman, Josepha. 1995. *Told Tales: Nine Folktales from Around the World*. New York: Silver Moon, pp. 9–13. 4 min.

The Witch of Rollright

Beset by an advancing king seeking to conquer his land, a young farmer approaches an ancient witch for help. He is surprised to find that the witch is neither old nor ugly. She has him welcome the king and his soldiers with provisions and then sets to work, enlisting the help of the fairy folk. The king and his guards are turned to stone, and the witch transforms herself into an elder tree to keep watch over the enemy. The resulting circle of stones is known as "The Rollrights"; to this day, it is impossible to count just how many stones there are in the circle.

> Matthews, John, and Caitlin Matthews. 1998. *The Wizard King and Other Spellbinding Tales*. New York: Barefoot Books, pp. 32–39. 11 min.

References

Aylwin, Tony. 1981. Using Myths and Legends in Schools. *Children's Literature in Education* 12(2): 82–89.

Egoff, Sheila. 1975. *The Republic of Childhood: A Critical Guide to Canadian Children's Literature in English*. 2d ed. Toronto: Oxford University Press.

Egoff, Sheila. 1981. *Thursday's Child: Trends and Patterns in Contemporary Children's Literature*. Chicago: American Library Association.

Eliade, Mircea. 1963. *Myth and Reality*. Vol. 31. World Perspectives. New York: Harper & Row.

Kraus, Anne Marie. 1998. *Folktale Themes and Activities for Children*. Volume I, *Pourquoi Tales*. Englewood, CO: Teacher Ideas Press.

Leeming, David Adams, ed. 1997. *Storytelling Encyclopedia: Historical, Cultural, and Multiethnic Approaches to Oral Traditions Around the World*. Phoenix, AZ: Oryx.

Stohler, Sara J. 1987. The Mythic World of Childhood. *Children's Literature Association Quarterly* 12(1): 28–32.

Sutherland, Zena, Dianne L. Monson, and May Hill Arbuthnot. 1981. *Children and Books*. 6th ed. Glenview, IL: Scott, Foresman.

Chapter 7

Tales of Laughter

"*Y*ou hear about that guy in Regina?" "What guy?"
"Went to get a tooth pulled out at the dentist, sat
back, opened his mouth, and in jumped a grasshopper. Nearly choked to death. Darnedest thing was, when
the grasshopper popped back out, it was holding the
tooth!"

—Arthur Slade, *Dust*

We all like to laugh. It is the "medicine" that helps us through trials and tribulations of everyday life. Young adults are no different. They love to have something strike them as funny, but often, because they have erected emotional
guards, the humor needs to sneak up and catch them unaware. Tales that are tall
and twisted fit the bill admirably, as do tales about fools and their exploits.

Tall Tales

"Like almost everyone, children respond to hyperbole in humor. Two in-
triguing forms are the tall tale, which is essentially a joke in slow motion, and the
lie, a related mode" (Schwartz 1977, 286). Junior high school student audiences
particularly enjoy the blatant humor of the tall tale juxtaposed with the deadpan
delivery that is part and parcel of the form. "The tall tale is a comic fiction disguised as fact, deliberately exaggerated to the limits of credibility or beyond in

order to reveal emotional truths, to awaken his audience, to exercise fears, to define and bind a social group" (Brown 1987, 1).

Printed versions of tall tales lack the impact, and often the humor, that is evident in oral transmission because the human element must be present to make the humor work. As Brunvand (1968) points out, "the art is primarily a verbal one, deriving from the skill of the teller rather than from the originality of his material" (116). This art depends on the pace of delivery ("never hurried, never dragged"), skillful timing, the dramatic use of the pause for emphasis, and drawing out the ending to deliver a more emphatic punch (Botkin 1975, 497). The success of tall tales also depends on a willingness to lie and to be lied to while keeping a straight face (Brunvand 1968, 116). The straight face and practiced nonreaction to external stimulus is a mechanism that young adults strive to maintain all the time. Encourage your students to tell tall tales, to research them or develop their own. Young adults appreciate permission to lie creatively.

Turn the students into tellers. Speaking formally before one's peers is extremely daunting for most young adults, but through various exercises and frequent practice, young adults (as well as any first-time teller) become more confident about public speaking and peer-group activities. Telling tall tales, being allowed to lie creatively before their peers, helps build confidence and self-esteem. A tall tale, like an urban legend, can be short and therefore is not as daunting as a longer tale.

In *Storytelling Activities*, Livo and Rietz encourage the stringing together of tall tales to produce a single tale. This activity is simplified by the fact that tall tales tend to cluster by topic. I followed their advice one year, developing a tall tale to tell for a Mother's Day program that I knew my own mother would be attending. Although I enjoyed developing it with the idea of surprising my mother with the tale, the actual telling of it and watching her face as I did so far surpassed my expectations. "My Mother's Pets," which can be found in full text in Chapter 9, was a marriage of two traditional tall tales, a little family history, and some natural history. It became my mother's story, and when she heard different versions from other tellers, she would argue that they told it wrong! The funniest aspect of this successful Mother's Day gift was when my mother asked me to tell it at a family reunion dinner. I did not want to do this because I knew what would happen, and it did—members of her family tried to place it in historical context, trying to remember the incident that must have taken place in their childhood as well, totally missing the exaggeration, the ridiculousness of it all. I encourage young adult audiences to follow my example—to create inexpensive gifts for their parents and other loved ones—and include them in a story.

Twists and Turns

Young adults relish stories that offer twists on traditional tales and conventional endings. Comprehension of a traditional story presented from a different point of view requires an intellectual skill that is not reached until approximately age twelve (Horner 1983, 461). Young adults particularly enjoy stories in which their predictions of outcome are led in one direction by the action and then foiled by the surprise ending or twist in the plot.

Young adults, particularly at ages twelve and thirteen, are intensely interested in practical jokes and enjoy the trickster stories that are found in every folklore tradition. Traditional trickster tales play an important role. They represent chaos in the ordered life and poke fun at the illusions of people (Yolen 1986, 125). Trickster characters and plot twists found in literary tales today perform the same functions. On the other hand, older young adults have developed a more subtle humor and appreciate satire, parody, and witticism (Nilsen and Donelson 1985, 336).

Numbskulls and Other Fools

Numbskull tales is a generic term for the absurdity, ignoramus, noodle, and fool stories that are prolific universally. They are humorous stories of a semi-sophisticated type. "The butts of these stories are stupid peasants, city slickers, absent-minded professors, Little Morons, habitual worriers" (Leach 1972, 797). The tales are a distinct genre but do blend into trickster tales, where the dupes of the tricksters are considered numbskulls. The numbskull stories resemble the tall tale in humor and exaggeration but are usually shorter, with a focus on a single situation. The main character in a numbskull tale is the butt of the joke.

Martha Hamilton and Mitch Weiss, in their introduction to *Noodlehead Stories: World Tales Kids Can Read and Tell,* enumerate some of the ways the characters are foolish in this type of story. The main characters can be well meaning and literal, following directions blindly without any evidence of critical thinking; they can look for the most complicated solution to any problem causing all types of grief for themselves in the process; they can be of either gender (although, like tall tales, male characters figure largely as main characters in these tales) and from any economic background (Hamilton and Weiss 2000). These stories are often far-fetched and are told to entertain, not to make fun of others. "What a comfort to think that we just do small foolish things now and then, while others are capable of such lunacy" (Hamilton and Weiss 2000, 14).

Annotated Bibliography

Ali the Persian

Ali tells the Caliph Harun Al-Rashid a story about his own travels when he ventured away from Baghdad and became the victim of a thief. The thief and Ali then both tried to establish their ownership of the stolen leather bag, with hilarious results.

> Baltuck, Naomi, reteller. 1995. *Apples from Heaven: Multicultural Folk Tales about Stories and Storytellers*. North Haven, CT: Linnet, pp. 22–25. 7 min. Adapted from Richard Burton's "Tale of Ali the Persian" in *The Book of the Thousand Nights and a Night* (1885–1888).

An Amazing Long Time

Fifteen-year-old Weldon rebelled against his father when sent out to fetch a log from the woodpile. He just kept walking and did not return for six years. When he came back, he decided to have a little fun and so walked in the house with a log just as his father had instructed him to do so many years before. All the bemused father could say was, "It took you an amazing long time to do so!"

> De Spain, Pleasant. 2000. *Sweet Land of Story: Thirty-Six American Tales to Tell*. Little Rock, AR: August House, pp. 22–24. 4 min. Also found in B. A. Botkin's *A Treasury of New England Folklore* (1947), 86.

Ashes for Sale

A sarcastic remark from a neighbor leads Pedro on an adventure. He receives a scary mask in trade, meets a band of robbers, and with the unplanned help of the mask, realizes his dream of becoming rich. He also has revenge on the neighbor.

> DeSpain, Pleasant. 1999. *The Emerald Lizard: Fifteen Latin American Tales to Tell in English and Spanish*. Little Rock, AR: August House, pp. 165–69. 5 min. Another version can be found in Grant Lyons' *Tales the People Tell in Mexico* (1972).

Beedanbun

Fishing guides have their own brand of humor! When a tourist tries to find out if there is a special Indian ceremony to ensure good fishing, Gilbert has no hesitation in offering him the bait of a "sacred" call to the fish.

> Wagamese, Richard. 1994. *Keeper'n Me*. Toronto: Doubleday Canada, pp. 84–87. 7 min. This is an excerpt from the novel about a young Native man who returns to the reserve for the first time since he was taken away as a young child. The novel is filled with stories about the characters that he meets during his journey to discover himself. Gilbert's story demonstrates that the "stoic Indian" may have a great sense of humor when dealing with "outsiders."

Buzzard and Wren Have a Race

Buzzard taunts Wren with his flying prowess until Wren proposes a race to see who can fly the highest. Buzzard lifts off but, unknown to him, has Wren as a passenger on his wing. Regardless of how high he flies, Buzzard can hear Wren's voice above him, and Wren is declared the winner.

Hamilton, Virginia. 1997. *A Ring of Tricksters: Animal Tales from America, the West Indies and Africa*. New York: Blue Sky Press, pp. 25–31. 4 min.

Dance Like Nobody Is Watching

Dave is always in a great mood, always making people laugh. He believed that life was about choices; people could choose to be a victim or to learn from their experiences. This attitude was tested to the limit the day Dave got shot during a robbery attempt at his place of work. When the doctors were despairing of his chance of survival, he made them laugh and taught them a lesson at the same time.

Livo, Norma J. 2001. *Story Medicine: Multicultural Tales of Healing and Transformation*. Englewood, CO: Libraries Unlimited, pp. 68–70. 5 min. The author identifies this tale as an urban myth.

The Dead Mule

When the white mule a trader was going to buy drops dead, the trader is a trifle bewildered about his next step. He decides to buy the mule anyway! When the original owner met up with the trader some time later, he discovered how the trader made money from the dead animal. He sold raffle tickets with the mule as the prize!

May, Jim, reteller. 1994. In *Ready-to-Tell Tales: Sure-Fire Stories from America's Favorite Storytellers*, edited by David Holt and Bill Mooney. Little Rock, AR: August House, pp. 130–32. 4 min.

The Dragon King's Feast

Two brothers, well known for their talent at telling tall tales, cannot stop trying to out tell each other. Their lifelong addiction is good natured and harmless, however.

Baltuck, Naomi, reteller. 1995. *Apples from Heaven: Multicultural Folk Tales about Stories and Storytellers*. North Haven, CT: Linnet, pp. 8–10. 3 min.

The Farmer Who Was Easily Fooled

Two thieves convince a farmer that one of them is his former donkey, transformed into a man because of good behavior, and walk away with the donkey and some money. They sell the donkey at the market. When the farmer sees it there, he is quite distraught: obviously the man could not behave properly and was once more in donkey form.

> Hamilton, Martha, and Mitch Weiss, 2000. *Noodlehead Stories: World Tales Kids Can Read and Tell*. Little Rock, AR: August House, pp. 26–28. 3 min.

Five Eggs

A poor husband and wife finally have a windfall—five eggs to share. Ah, but how do you share them equally? The wife goes to extreme lengths to have the extra egg in this amusing but touching tale.

> DeSpain, Pleasant. 1999. *The Emerald Lizard: Fifteen Latin American Tales to Tell in English and Spanish*. Little Rock, AR: August House, pp. 43–46. 4 min. Another version can be found in Harold Courlander's *Ride With the Sun: An Anthology of Folk Tales and Stories from the United Nations* (1955).

The Four Ne'er-Do-Wells

Four starving men raid a rich man's orchard and are caught red-handed. When the owner of the orchard demands to know who they are, the thieves answer respectively that they are a donkey, a fish, a sailor, and a nightingale. When the man demands to hear the nightingale's song, he is dismayed at the sour notes. His sense of humor jumps to the surface, however, and the four thieves are sent away with their stomachs full.

> Baltuck, Naomi, reteller. 1995. *Apples from Heaven: Multicultural Folk Tales about Stories and Storytellers*. North Haven, CT: Linnet, pp. 26–28. 4 min. Adapted from Pinhas Sadeh's *Jewish Folktales* (1989).

The Good Neighbor

An angry elderly man who claims the shade belongs to him accosts a young man sitting in the shade under a tree. To the amusement of the greedy old man, the young man buys the shade, but his amusement soon turns sour when the young man follows his shade into the old man's own house.

> Curry, Lindy Soon, reteller. 1999. *A Tiger by the Tail and Other Stories from the Heart of Korea*. Englewood, CO: Libraries Unlimited, pp. 51–53. 3 min.

The Good Wife

A clever wife cures her extremely lazy husband by first disguising herself as death and then as the "angel in charge of work for the dead."

> Kane, Alice, reteller. 1995. *The Dreamer Awakes*. Peterborough, ON: Broadview Press, pp. 101–103. 4 min. From George and Helen Papashvily's *Yes and No Stories: A Book of Georgian Folk Tales* (1946).

The Greedy Guest

When a greedy soldier chokes to death at the home of his captain, his hosts decide to move his body to the home of a doctor. When the horrified doctor finds the dead body on his doorstep, he decides to move it as well. The body is moved numerous times until it finally arrives at the temple. The priest confesses to the man's murder, but all of his neighbors rush to explain their participation in the matter. Finally, the chicken bone in the man's throat is dislodged, and everyone learns the man is not dead at all—but he is still greedy!

> Spagnoli, Cathy, and Paramasivam Samanna. 1999. *Jasmine and Coconuts: South Indian Tales*. Englewood, CO: Libraries Unlimited, pp. 43–45. 5 min. Adapted from retellings in *Tales of Tamil Nadu* (1985) and *Folk Tales of Tamilnadu* (1986). The author points out the similarities to "Old Drye Frye" in Richard Chase's *Grandfather Tales*, but with a different surprise twist in the ending (144).

Green Plague

A modern version of the Pied Piper story featuring frogs rather than the old rats.

> Yolen, Jane. 2000. In *Ribbiting Tales: Original Stories about Frogs*, edited by Nancy Springer. New York: Philomel, pp. 43–51. 8 min.

Hershele's Feast

When trickster Hershele Ostropolier is ridiculed, he sweetly takes his revenge by inviting his tormentors to a feast. After enjoying the scrumptious meal, his guests discover that they must pay for the entire celebration.

> Sherman, Josepha, reteller. 1996. *Trickster Tales: Forty Folk Stories from Around the World*. Little Rock, AR: August House, pp. 46–48. 4 min. "Tales about justice, even such tricky justice as Hershele gains, are popular in Jewish folklore, as are humorous tales" (151).

Hodja

The Hodja has a contest of strength with the town bully. Needless to say, the Hodja proves his wisdom is much stronger than brute strength.

> Spagnoli, Cathy. 1998. *Asian Tales and Tellers*, Little Rock, AR: August House, pp. 160–61. 1 min.

How Hare Drank Boiling Water and Married the Beautiful Princess

The king decided that whoever could drink boiling water from a cauldron would win his daughter's hand. All of the animals tried, but none could get close enough to attempt the feat because of the hot steam that rose from the cauldron. Hare, a great storyteller, uses his gift and gains a princess. This story dramatizes the power of storytelling.

> Mama, Raouf, translator and reteller. 1998. *Why Goats Smell Bad and Other Stories from Benin*. North Haven, CT: Linnet, pp. 95–99. 5 min.

How the Order Was Obeyed

This is a tale from Croatia in which an ordinary citizen following the direct words of the law defies the oppressive Turkish official's orders. Everyone had to carry a lantern, but there was no directive that the lantern had to have a candle or that it be lit!

> Marshall, Bonnie C., reteller. 2001. *Tales from the Heart of the Balkans*. Englewood, CO: Libraries Unlimited, pp. 131–32. 3 min.

Justice Is Blind

A peasant sells his one cow several times to various people who all ask him to deliver the cow to their homes. When the cow does not materialize, the victims take the peasant to court. The lawyer tells him to answer all questions with the same nonsensical phrase, "Waank, Waank, Waank." The lawyer wins the case for his client, but does he get paid for his services? "Waank, Waank, Waank!"

> Parent, Michael, and Julien Oliver, retellers. 1996. *Of Kings and Fools: Stories of the French Tradition in North America*. Little Rock, AR: August House, pp. 75–78. 6 min. Translated and adapted from Marius Barbeau's *Les reves des chasseurs (The Dreams of the Hunters;* 1945)

Malindy and Little Devil

Malindy loved to sing and dance. One day while dancing and carrying a pail of milk, she spilt it all over herself. She commenced to crying but quickly stopped when offered a deal with a little devil. She promised her soul for a full pail of milk, a clean and dry dress, and twenty-nine years on earth. By the time the devil returned, Malindy had forgotten the deal, but a promise is a promise! So Malindy tore off the sole of her shoe and gave it to him.

> Hamilton, Virginia. 1995. *Her Stories: African American Folktales, Fairy Tales and True Tales*. New York: Blue Sky, pp. 61–65. 5 min.

One Sad Story

After the elevator breaks down, three students decide to walk up sixty flights of stairs to their dormitory, telling each other stories to help the climb go more quickly. They make it to the fifty-ninth floor when they hear the saddest story of them all—the key to the room is back in their classroom!

> Spagnoli, Cathy, and Paramasivam Samanna. 1999. *Jasmine and Coconuts: South Indian Tales*. Englewood, CO: Libraries Unlimited, p. 128. 1 min.

The Orphan and the Miser

The miser takes in a young orphan boy to work for him and promises that one day the boy may wed his daughter. Although the young couple fall in love, the miser refuses to allow his daughter to marry such a poor man.

The miser takes the young man to his cousin the judge to pay for even contemplating the thought of marriage. The judge rules against the young man but neither he nor the miser realize the cleverness and love of the young couple until it is too late.

Sherman, Josepha 1994. *Once Upon a Galaxy: The Ancient Stories behind Star Wars, Superman and Other Popular Fantasies*. Little Rock, AR: August House, pp. 207–10. 5 min. Retold from the *Sandalwood Box: Folktales from Tadzikistan* translated by Katya Sheppard.

The Passing of the Eye

While on a quest a hero comes upon three blind old women who are arguing. He follows the quest manual to the hilt, but he probably should have studied his Greek mythology instead!

Yolen, Jane. 1994. *Here There Be Witches*. San Diego, CA: Harcourt Brace Jovanovich, pp. 25–26. 3 min.

The Queen of the Bees

In this tale, adapted from the Brothers Grimm, three princesses are sent on a quest to find their fortune, break a spell, and to find princes to marry each of them. (But they were really sent on this quest to get them out of the castle—the two eldest were much too rude for words.) Following the traditional pattern of these tales, the youngest sister does all the work, makes all the right connections with a bevy of supernatural helpers, and eventually succeeds for all three of them. The two older princesses may be in for a surprise when they meet their princely prizes, however.

French, Vivian. 1997. In *Breaking the Spell: Tales of Enchantment*. Selected by Sally Grindley. New York: Kingfisher, 34–46. 12 min.

A Real Bargain

In this Hodja story from southern India, where the Hodja is known as Khwaja Nasruddin, the Hodja helps the innkeeper with an obnoxious guest.

Spagnoli, Cathy, and Paramasivam Samanna. 1999. *Jasmine and Coconuts: South Indian Tales*. Englewood, CO: Libraries Unlimited, p. 123. 1 min.

A Sackful of Stories

Hans agrees to herd the king's rabbits in exchange for the hand of the princess. He is equipped with a magic whistle that recovers all things lost. When the king initially reneges on his promise, Hans agrees to herd the rabbits again and again. The royal family attempt to make a fool of Hans, but to no avail; then Hans discloses their duplicity in a storytelling contest. His reward is a bride, and the kingdom with an annual storytelling festival.

Baltuck, Naomi, reteller. 1995. *Apples from Heaven: Multicultural Folk Tales about Stories and Storytellers*. North Haven, CT: Linnet, pp. 58–68. 12 min.

The Smuggler

When Nasrudin continuously takes his donkeys back and forth across the border, the guards know that he is smuggling something. But, as hard as they look, they can find nothing. Years later, the captain of the guards discovers the truth. A modern retelling of this story was recommended in *Storytelling for Young Adults* (68).

DeSpain, Pleasant, reteller. 2001. *Tales of Tricksters*. Vol. 1, The Books of Nine Lives. Little Rock, AR: August House, pp. 19–23. 3 min. From Idries Shah's *Mulla Nasrudin* (1972).

The Storekeeper

The people of his community convince a less than trustworthy shopkeeper to attend the revival meeting, hoping to get him to mend his ways. The teachings that he takes home with him are not quite what the community had envisioned. A tall tale from the American south.

McConnell, Doc, reteller. 1994. In *Ready-to-Tell Tales: Sure-Fire Stories from America's Favorite Storytellers*, edited by David Holt and Bill Mooney. Little Rock, AR: August House, pp. 86–90. 5 min.

The Thief Who Aimed to Please

When accosted by a thief, a traveler asks him to make sure the robbery looked convincing to his wife by shooting a hole in his jacket and then his hat. When the bullets run out, well, so does the thief's luck.

Hamilton, Martha, and Mitch Weiss, retellers. 2001. *Through the Grapevine: World Tales Kids Can Read and Tell*. Little Rock, AR: August House, pp. 50–51. 2 min.

Ti-Jean Joins the Elite

Ti-Jean wants nothing more than to become a member of the elite. Following his mother's advice, he decides to become a doctor. He learns a lot of large words, collects plants and herbs, and begins his career. He finds himself at a nearby castle where he promises to cure all ailments for the reward of half the kingdom, the princess' hand in marriage, and great wealth. He prepares the cure by informing the people that they must first find the sickest person among them, who will be then boiled in a cauldron to make a healing potion the rest of them will drink. As Ti-Jean waits patiently for the sickest person to step forward, all sorts of cures take place as the people begin to feel better than they ever had before! He is rewarded but quickly squanders his wealth and the princess' patience. Finally, he returns home to his mother, not at all wealthy and, most probably, not very wise either.

Parent, Michael and Julien Oliver, retellers. 1996. *Of Kings and Fools: Stories of the French Tradition in North America*. Little Rock, AR: August House, pp. 38–44. 8 min.

Trust

A poor rag picker entrusts his meager savings to a judge, but when he goes to collect them, the judge denies any knowledge of the savings. A wealthy woman witnesses the poor man's despair. After listening to his story, she tricks the judge into returning the man's money. The judge recognizes the woman's cleverness and has a good laugh himself.

Spagnoli, Cathy. 2001. *Terrific Trickster Tales from Asia*. Fort Atkinson, WI: Alleyside Press, pp. 70–71. 3 min. The story came from Sultan Ali, Cholamandal, India, 1977.

Tyl Eulenspiegel and the Marvelous Painting

Tyl promises to paint the portraits of prominent people in the court. They threaten to kill him if he does not make them look perfect, and his patron threatens the same unless Tyl paints them exactly as they are. Tyl manages to do both, without doing anything at all. This story has strong echoes of Hans Christian Andersen's "The Emperor's New Clothes."

Sherman, Josepha, reteller. 1996. *Trickster Tales: Forty Folk Stories from Around the World*. Little Rock, AR: August House, pp. 40–42. 4 min.

What Gold?

Charles Withington leaves his wife alone when he must travel, even though the notorious Anderson Gang is in the neighborhood. The Andersons heard about the couple's gold and decide to steal it while Charles is away. When they arrive at the homestead, Mrs. Withington is on the front porch doing laundry in a huge washtub. The robbers search the entire house and yard but leave the farm in disgust when they find no evidence of the gold they had heard about. A story about the positive side of laundering money!

De Spain, Pleasant. 2000. *Sweet Land of Story: Thirty-Six American Tales to Tell*. Little Rock, AR: August House, pp. 22–24. 4 min.

Who Will Buy My Horse?

When Martin's favorite horse disappears, he rashly announces that he is only concerned about the horse's well-being. In fact, if the horse returns, he will sell him for $1. He simply wants to make sure the horse is alright. The horse returns and Martin sets out to keep his promise, he will only sell it to the person who buys his mangy old dog for $500.

DeSpain, Pleasant, reteller. 2001. *Tales of Wisdom and Justice*. Vol. 3, The Books of Nine Lives. Little Rock, AR: August House, pp. 61–65. 5 min.

Whose Horse Is Whose?

Two fools can not tell the difference between their two horses and spend a lot of thought and energy trying to figure it out. This simple tale demonstrates that the answer to a problem is often obvious but overlooked because people do not pay attention.

Hamilton, Martha, and Mitch Weiss, 2000. *Noodlehead Stories: World Tales Kids Can Read and Tell*. Little Rock, AR: August House, pp. 38–39. 1 min.

Witchfinder

A man whose cows have suddenly gone dry suspects a witch has cursed him. He goes to the witchfinder and soon discovers the woman behind the spell. A story from the Isle of Skye, told from several perspectives, with a twist at the end.

Yolen, Jane. 1994. *Here There Be Witches*. San Diego, CA: Harcourt Brace Jovanovich, pp. 110–15. 7 min.

References

Botkin, B. A. 1975. *A Treasury of Western Folklore*. Rev. ed. New York: Crown.

Brown, Carolyn S. 1987. *The Tall Tale in American Folklore and Literature*. Knoxville, TN: University of Tennessee Press.

Brunvand, Jan Harold. 1968. *The Study of American Folklore: An Introduction*. New York: W. W. Norton.

Horner, Beth. 1983. To Tell or Not to Tell: Storytelling for Young Adults. *Illinois Libraries* 65(7): 458–64.

Leach, Maria, ed. 1984. *Funk & Wagnall's Standard Dictionary of Folklore, Mythology, and Legend*. San Francisco: Harper.

Livo, Norma J., and Sandra A. Rietz. 1987. *Storytelling Activities*. Englewood, CO: Libraries Unlimited.

Hamilton, Martha, and Mitch Weiss, 2000. *Noodlehead Stories: World Tales Kids Can Read and Tell*. Little Rock, AR: August House.

Nilsen, Alleen Pace, and Kenneth L. Donelson. 1985. *Literature for Today's Young Adults*. 2d ed. Glenview, IL: Scott, Foresman.

Schwartz, Alvin. 1977. Children, Humor and Folklore. *The Horn Book* 53(3): 281–87.

Yolen, Jane. 1986. *Favorite Folktales from Around the World*. New York: Pantheon.

Chapter 8

Tales of the Arts and Sciences

I selected the stories for this chapter with possible school curricula directly in mind. While they can be told for sheer entertainment pleasure, these tales also demonstrate mathematical or scientific principles, inform listeners of the meanings behind words and phrases, and help them discover music and musical instruments, among other things. The suggested stories in this chapter also derive from folklore, from stories of life experiences, and from literature but, in contrast to previous chapters, focus more on the creation than on the characters. Because of possible connections to the classroom, I have included more background information on the tales and lessons than I have in the previous chapters. Young adults have a wide variety of interests and appreciate stories that celebrate the achievements of people much like themselves. These tales may be the creation of an author or the result of creativity in another sphere such as mathematics or music. Young adults also delight in discovering the story behind something they may have considered ordinary—or may not have considered at all—such as the formation of a common word or phrase in their everyday speech.

Literary Tales

*A*nil needed to comfort herself with old friends, sentences from books, voices she could trust.

—Michael Ondaatje, *Anil's Ghost*

Literary tales begin as written rather than oral tales and are the creation of an identifiable author. "The only person with the authority to infuse the written story with its correct oral language features is the author" (Livo and Rietz 1986, 152). Livo and Rietz discuss how the written story is meant to be read and not heard, but many authors have created stories that cry out to be told. Nonetheless, literary tales are all protected by copyright and usually cannot be adapted freely by a storyteller; instead they must be memorized and delivered in the author's own words. It is necessary to obtain permission to tell these tales. In many cases, if the storyteller earns a fee with the story, the author expects remuneration. A letter requesting permission to use the story should be written to the author or literary agent. Publishers will pass on requests to their authors, but they usually wait until they have a batch of requests rather than forwarding them individually. The letter must include the title of the story as well as the plans the storyteller has for the story. The author has to be informed how the story is to be used and if any adaptation of the story is being considered. The letter should state whether the story will be told in schools and libraries or performed on a stage, whether the storyteller is telling the story as part of his or her occupation (teacher, librarian, hospital aide), and whether the storyteller will be paid for the performances (Yolen 1987, 7).

The author must be credited every time the story is told. If you distribute handouts, include bibliographic information on each literary tale that you use in the program. If possible, display the books that incorporate the stories.

Excerpts from longer works are often told to introduce the book from which they are taken or to introduce the body of work of a particular author. Often the audience must be given background information before the story can be told to place it in context. Frequently they request additional information after the telling and will wish to read the book.

Fractured Fairy Tales

In the past decade, fractured fairy tales have flourished, with authors rearranging the plots of traditional tales to create new plots with essentially different messages. "Fractured fairy tales are closely related to fairy-tale parodies, but the two serve different purposes: parodies mock individual tales and the genre as a whole; fractured fairy tales, with a reforming intent, seek to impart updated social and moral messages" (Zipes 2000, 172). Although some of the more oral fractured fairy tales are included in this chapter, I suggest that readers refer to Anna Altmann's and my research on the most pertinent fractured fairy tales for young adults of the most popular folk tales in our two books, *New Tales for Old* and *Tales, Then and Now*.

Word Origins

*I*n the beginning, Odysseus was just a man like any man. But he went on a long, dangerous journey, much as we are doing, and people spoke of it for generations, until eventually he became a myth. Later his adventures were written down in a book, and his name became the word for "long, adventurous journey." Odyssey.

—Rodman Philbrick, *The Last Book in the Universe*

One of my prime concerns in my storytelling classes at the university is to make sure that my students are aware of the legacy of these old tales. The words we speak and write are often based on folklore. We take for granted the names of the days of the week and the months of the year, but few of us realize that the majority of them are based on classical mythology. Other adjectives, adverbs, nouns, verbs, and figures of speech also have their roots in ancient tales. I explore several of these in more detail later in the discussion.

Scientific terminology is also heavily weighted in mythology. Chemical elements reminded their discoverers of mythical beings, so cobalt is named after the *kobalts* of German folklore, who were in the habit of tricking people in their underworld environment. This word was chosen because the element itself "tricked" the miners attempting to bring it to the surface. Iridium is named after *Iris,* the Greek goddess of the rainbow, because of the colors inherent in the compound. The Norse god of Thunder, Thor, gave his name to the element thorium because of its heavy radioactive nature as well as to Thursday (Thors-day). The stories behind these words enliven a science class but also make these terms more memorable to the students.

Animal and plant classification systems and names reflect the wider world of folklore as well. Spiders are known as *Arachnida*, named after Arachne and her misguided weaving contest with the Greek goddess, Athena.

Arachne, an extremely talented weaver, was very proud of her accomplishments. She bragged that she was a better weaver than even the goddess of wisdom and the arts and sciences. The angry goddess, Athena herself, appeared in the guise of an old woman at Arachne's door. When she could not convince Arachne of her superior talent, Athena threw off her disguise and challenged the young weaver to a contest. Although fearful of the angry goddess, Arachne was convinced of her own proficiency, and she quickly and skillfully wove into her tapestry countless stories of the errors and misdeeds of the gods. This further angered the goddess who tore Arachne's work into a web of tatters. Devastated by

this action and the strength of Athena's displeasure, Arachne hung herself in grief. A calmer Athena then transformed Arachne into a spider so
that she could continue to weave.

Natural phenomena have also been explained through the use of ancient
myths, and these tales live on with the continued use of these terms. Echo and
Narcissus's story gave rise to the naming of the narcissus flower as well as to the
echo in empty rooms and in the mountains. The story of the infatuated nymph
and oblivious hunter is found in almost every collection of Greek myths and is
taught in upper elementary classes.

Stories Behind the Days of the Week

The naming of the days of the week in both English and French have always
fascinated me with their connections to the pantheon of gods from classical mythology.

The Greeks named the days of the week after the sun, the moon, and the five
known planets, which were named after the gods Ares, Hermes, Zeus, Aphro-
dite, and Cronus. The Romans substituted their equivalent gods for the Greek
ones: Mars, Mercury, Jupiter, Venus, and Saturn. The Norse equivalents were
substituted within their culture as well—Tiu, Woden, Thor, and Freya, although
they did not substitute Saturn. The presumed connections among the different
gods (and the days of the week) can be seen in the following chart.

Young adults should be familiar with the stories of the gods and goddesses
that they obliquely refer to every day. "Woden's Wagon" in Chapter 9 revolves
around Wednesday's namesake, Woden. Research reveals that Woden is usually
regarded as the head god among the ancient Anglo-Saxons by virtue that there
are far more references to Woden in Old English literature than any other god or
goddess. He was known as the god of death, battle, wisdom, the discoverer of the
runes and leader of the Wild Hunt. He was pictured as walking the landscape in
cloak and hood when the weather was fine, one-eyed and wise beyond all knowing. "But on dark and stormy nights he racketed across the sky at the head of his
wild hunt of lost and noisy souls" (Branston 1974, 97).

He is identified with the Norse god Odin, and, like his counterpart, besides
being the god of war and death, he is also the god of poetry, magic, and wisdom.
He is also known as Wotan in Richard Wagner's *Ring of the Nibelung*. There is,
interestingly, a strong similarity between Woden and Tolkien's character
Gandalf in *Lord of the Rings*. Gandalf's name, by the way, is found in the *Edda*.
Woden has long been identified with the Roman god Mercury because of the
gods' connection with the leading of the souls of the dead, evidenced by the
French word for Wednesday, Mercredi, or Mercury's day (Branston 1974, 96).

The Stories behind the Days of the Week

Modern English	Middle English	Greek	Roman Deity	Norse/ Saxon Deity	Latin	French	Attribute of the God
Sunday	Sone (n) day or sun (nen) day	hemera heli(o)u			Dies solis	Dimanche	The Sun's Day
Monday	Mone(n) day	Hemera Selenes			Dies lunae	Lundi	The Moon's Day
Tuesday	Tiwesday or Tewesday	Hemera Areos (day of Ares)	Mars	Tui	Dies Martis (day of Mars)	Mardi	Tui is the god of war and the sky; Ares and Mars are also gods of war.
Wednesday	Wodenesday	Hemera Hermu (day of Hermes)	Mercury	Odin/ Woden	Dies Mercurii (day of Mercury)	Mecredi	Woden is the chief Anglo-Saxon god. Mercury (Roman) and Hermes (Greek) are the messenger gods.
Thursday	Thur(s) day	Hemera Dios (day of Zeus)	Jupiter or Jove	Thor	Dies Jovis (day of Jupiter)	Jeudi	Thor is the Norse god of thunder. Jupiter, the supreme Roman god is noted for creating thunder and lightning.
Friday	Fridai or Friegdaeg	Hemera Aphrodite (day of Aphrodite)	Venus	Freya (Fria)	Dies Veneris (day of Venus)	Vendredi	Freya is the goddess of love, beauty and leader of the Valkyries. Aphrodite (Greek) and Venus (Roman) are goddesses of love and beauty.
Saturday	Saterday	Hemera Khronu (day of Chronus)	Saturn		Dies Saturni (day of Saturn)	Samedi	Saturn is the god of agriculture. Chronus is the Greek god who ruled the universe until dethroned by his son Zeus.

Stories behind the other days of the week and the months of the year can be found in various collections of classical mythology. I recommend that young adults research the myths and develop their own tales to illuminate their understanding of why these particular gods and goddesses were chosen to be remembered in our daily calendar of events.

Other Etymologies

I have long recommended that students of writing also study etymology, the meaning behind our words. Once one knows the story of a word, the word becomes more of an entity, something that cannot be easily discarded or displaced with a thesaurus entry!

Sometimes a word becomes part of our language because of failed scientific experiments. For example, the word "galvanize" means to stimulate or shock with an electrical current or to jolt into action, as if by electric shock. The eighteenth-century physiologist Luigi Galvani, while dissecting a frog, noticed that when an exposed nerve was touched with his scalpel, the frog's leg twitched. The scientist theorized that nerves produce electricity and that the scalpel served as an electrical conductor. Galvani began a long series of experiments to test his hypothesis. He discovered that his original idea was faulty; the frog's nerves had been shocked into motion by the scalpel that had become accidentally charged when resting beside an electrical instrument. Although his idea was erroneous, his research launched a new field of study on generating electricity by chemical means and inspired the word *galvanize.* It is thought that Galvani's experiments also inspired Mary Shelley's novel, *Frankenstein: Or, the Modern Prometheus.* The story behind the inspiration for this novel can be found as a story for the telling in "The Curious Dream" annotated in this chapter.

Other words arrive because of metaphoric images. When Portuguese explorers first sighted coconuts, they were amazed at the resemblance between the three holes in the bottom of the nut and a tiny face. They immediately referred to the fruit as "coco," the Portuguese word for goblin or grinning skull. English speakers added the appellation, nut to the Portuguese, and it entered our lexicon.

Numerous words evolve from our literature. The word *canter,* a smooth easy gait for horse that is faster than a trot but slower than a gallop can trace its origin to the twelfth century.

After the murder of Thomas Becket in England's Canterbury Cathedral in the twelfth century, Canterbury became a popular destination for countless religious pilgrims traveling on horseback, including those described in Chaucer's *Canterbury Tales.* By the early seventeenth century, the expression "Canterbury pace" had come to mean the easy gait at which these faithful rode to their destination. By 1673, Canterbury had become a verb, and by 1706, had shortened to "canter." (Barnette, n.d.)

Numerous other words and sayings came from the pen of William Shakespeare. Although some of these are generously attributed to him, the fact that others were borrowed from folklore may not be as widely realized. One of the most famous is the adjective "puckish," which means mischievous or impish. In folklore, the *pouke* referred to an evil, malicious spirit but under the influence of Shakespeare's pen, the trickster of *A Midsummer Night's Dream* was reborn and rehabilitated.

A more involved reworking of a Jewish folktale gave *Merchant of Venice* its form and the English language a popular phrase. Colin Swatridge, in an editorial in *The Hindu Online,* refers to this play when he asks the question, what is the difference between law and justice?

> Perhaps the most expressive example of the distinction in literature is provided by Shakespeare in *The Merchant of Venice*. Antonio, the merchant, borrows money from the moneylender Shylock. So certain is Antonio of imminent wealth that, "in merry sport," he signs a bond to repay the money, or surrender a pound of his flesh. When misfortune strikes, and he cannot repay the loan, Shylock demands his pound of flesh. The demand is unjust, grotesque, out of proportion; but the law is on his side. Even Portia, Antonio's beloved, disguised as a lawyer has to concede this: "the Venetian law cannot impugn you as you proceed." A contract is a contract. There is no power in Venice can alter a degree established." The only way in which Portia can save Antonio from the surgeon's knife, is to take the law literally, and have Shylock's legal claim rebound on him. (33)

The idiom "a pound of flesh" has come to mean a debt for which payment is harshly insisted upon and one that must follow the exact terms of the agreement, the *bond literatim et verbatim.* It is one that is often used in articles and arguments such as the one quoted here. When asking young adults about the origin of the phrase, those who knew the play identified the scene, but no one realized that the theme of the pound of flesh has much more ancient roots then that. In Chapter 9, I have included a version of a Jewish folktale that may have been making the rounds when Shakespeare was creating his play. Those who defend this play from anti-Semitic charges often claim that Shakespeare did not know any Jews, but no one says anything about him knowing old stories.

Annotated Bibliography

The Beggar King

"To prevent Asmodeus, the Demon King, from stopping the construction of the holy temple, King Solomon captured Asmodeus and imprisoned him in a dungeon. The tale of 'The Beggar King' takes place upon the completion of the temple, when Asmodeus is about to be set free" (Forest 1995, 154). King Solomon is seeking the difference between truth and illusion and Asmodeus aids him in his discovery.

> Forest, Heather, reteller. 1995. *Wonder Tales from Around the World*. Little Rock, AR: August House, pp. 131–33. 4 min.

Can You Save the Day?

When the maiden Adononsi is captured by the rainbow snake, who plans to force her to marry him, her three friends rescue her. At the celebration feast, the friends each argue that Adononsi should marry him because of his efforts in rescuing her. The decision is finally left to Adononsi. Who does she choose? Can you help her and save the day?

> Mama, Raouf, translator and reteller. 1998. *Why Goats Smell Bad and Other Stories from Benin*. North Haven, CT: Linnet, pp. 60–66. 6 min. The python is one of the gods in the Fon pantheon. This tale is designed to test the wisdom of listeners and to spark a debate about a problem that has no obvious or easy solution. The most important point of the story may be that nothing lasts forever and that even the closest friendships come under strain sometimes (66).

The Captain's Goose

While waiting for his goose dinner, the sea captain and a wizard strike a deal to make the sea captain the king. The wizard challenges the sea captain to rid the land of a group of pirates. He does so easily, is crowned king and rules wisely until he refuses to pay the wizard for his help. The wizard immediately takes him back to the time before he met the wizard and was awaiting his dinner of a cooked goose. No longer a king, the sea captain realizes that "His goose has been cooked." "For when your goose is cooked, there is always a lesson to be learned" (13).

> Walker, Richard, reteller. 1998. *The Barefoot Book of Pirates*. New York: Barefoot Books, pp. 6–13. 7 min. From Gwen Jones's *Scandinavian Legends and Folktales* (1956).

Chanticleer and the Fox

The famous fable about the price of vanity concerns the rooster Chanticleer, his dream, the hen Pertelote and the flattering and hungry fox.

Osborne, Mary Pope, reteller. 1998. *Favorite Medieval Tales.* New York: Scholastic, pp. 67–72. 7 min. From Geoffrey Chaucer's *Canterbury Tales* (1386).

The Clever Wife

The uncle of a fourteen-year-old boy from an upper-class family cannot get him to learn a thing. Because the boy's father has already disowned him for the same reason, the uncle feels responsible for the good-natured child. When the boy grows older, the uncle arranges a marriage with a young woman, who also becomes upset when she sees that her husband does not read or study. She realizes that he loves stories and begins telling him tales. To her amazement, he easily remembers the stories she tells and, because he is hungry for more, she teaches him to read and then study for enjoyment. Eventually he takes his examinations and passes them with flying colors, becomes reunited with his family, and eventually is elected prime minister. But no matter how successful he becomes, he always credits his wife for his success.

Curry, Lindy Soon, reteller. 1999. *A Tiger by the Tail and Other Stories from the Heart of Korea.* Englewood, CO: Libraries Unlimited, pp. 69–72. 6 min. Traditionally, if you were a male from an aristocratic family in Korea, your job would be to study literature, pass the examination and become a government bureaucrat. "It is his own wife, a woman of humble origin, and not his male tutors of Neo-Confucian classics, who understands the fascinating dualism of literacy and orality, writing versus speaking, and reading versus hearing" (xviii).

A very similar tale from China, "The Mirror," is also annotated in this chapter.

The Curious Dream

Initially created to introduce Mary Shelley's famous novel, *Frankenstein,* to high school students, this story relates some of the author's early history and the curious dream that inspired her to write the novel.

Roe, Betty, Suellen Alfred, and Sandy Smith. (1998). *Teaching through Stories: Yours, Mine and Theirs.* Norwood, MA: Christopher-Gordon, pp. 84–85. 3 min. "Students are especially intrigued by the prospect of reading *Frankenstein* when they are told that Shelley wrote it when she was nineteen years old and that she was the first person to write science fiction" (84).

Enchanted Hotel

In this excerpt from the novel *echo,* we meet the protagonist's parents and follow their rather exotic courtship from their first meeting to their realization of their love for each other. Block's characters virtually emerge from the page.

Block, Francesca Lia. 2001. *echo.* New York: Joanna Cotler, pp. 47–59. 8 min.

The Feathered Snake: How Music Came to the World

When the world was created, an important element was missing: music. Quetzalcoatl was sent to get music from the selfish sun for those on earth. He brought back the musicians, who taught every creature they met how to sing or make and play flutes.

> Mayo, Margaret, reteller. 1996. *Mythical Birds and Beasts from Many Lands*. New York: Dutton, pp. 67–73. 10 min. Based on a poem from a sixteenth-century manuscript in Nahuatl, the language of the Aztecs and of the Toltecs before them. The quetzal is a bird that lives in the remote rain forests of southern Mexico and Guatemala. *Coatl* means snake. Thus Quetzalcoatl is a bird-snake, primarily a wind god and creator (107).

Food for Thought

A rich sheik, wounded and hungry, offers eight pieces of gold for eight loaves of bread. The distribution of the eight pieces of gold demonstrates three types of division: simple division, exact division, and perfect division.

> Tahan, Malba. 1993. *The Man Who Counted: A Collection of Mathematical Adventures*. Translated by Leslie Clark and Alastair Reid. New York: W. W. Norton, pp. 15–18. 6 min.

The Girl Who Couldn't Walk

A girl who cannot walk is happy, but her parents cannot accept her affliction and so begin looking for doctors to help her. One day a crippled old woman arrives at the house. She grants one wish to each of the three members of the family with the warning that the wish must be kept in their hearts. Once it is spoken, the wish will be broken. The mother immediately declares her wish and thus wastes it. The husband likewise wastes his wish, but the daughter uses hers to wish to be just like the old woman, who in reality is a magic hare. The girl's wish is quickly granted, and off the two hares run.

> Doherty, Berlie. 1997. *Tales of Wonder and Magic*. Cambridge, MA: Candlewick, pp. 93–100. 9 min.

A Ghost of an Affair

A romantic ghost story, or a romance story that features a ghost, or the story of how a ghost reaches through time to set a romance in motion. A ghost story for romantics rather than lovers of terror.

> Yolen, Jane. 2000. *Sister Emily's Lightship and Other Stories*. New York: TOR, pp. 251–66. 16 min.

A Gown of Moonthreads

The princess hears Jacob sobbing below her window, and upon hearing his tale of woe, decides to help him. She refers to the lessons from an old

Jewish folktale to give her inspiration. She attends the court dressed as Jacob's lawyer—a man—and successfully argues his case. When she reveals her identity to her young man, there is great rejoicing —and a marriage, the result of a clever and a courageous princess and a gown of moonthreads.

> Husain, Shahrukh. 1995. *Handsome Heroines: Women as Men in Folklore*, New York: Anchor, pp. 175–88. 20 min. See "A Pound of Flesh" in Chapter 9. The author used the same source and interwove her tale with fragments from a second Jewish folktale, "A Garment for the Moon." (From Howard Schwartz's *Miriam's Tambourine* (1988). The author asserts that Shakespeare's retelling was certainly based on one of the variants of this older tale. "Interestingly Shakespeare keeps the form of a Jewish money lender and an non-Jewish savior heroine, though the hero had to be a Gentile to make the story acceptable to a Christian audience highly suspicious of Jews in a society where intermarriage was frowned upon even between Christians of different denominations" (261).

Indian Summer

Zimo is a good farmer, but one year when he is ill, he does not have a chance to plant his crops. He goes to Gluskabe for help and is able to plant and harvest his crops in a brief period during the autumn. Since that time, there has always been a time of warm weather just before the snows. The Penobscot call it "A Person's Summer," but it is known to most as "Indian Summer" (45).

> Bruchac, Joseph, reteller. 1995. *Native Plant Stories*. Golden, CO: Fulcrum, pp. 43–45. 2 min. This is just one story relating the origin of this weather pattern. There are countless other theories of how the phrase originated. The earliest documented use of the term is 1778 in a letter from St. John de Crevecoeur.

The King and the Wrestler

A wrestler, looking for work, tells the king that he can walk with a large mountain on his head. Impressed, the king hires him, but when he asks the wrestler to do the deed, the wrestler informs the king that he did not say that he could pick up the mountain and place it on his head. He is willing to walk with it as soon as someone can place it on his head! This story demonstrates the wisdom of listening to what is actually being said.

> Hamilton, Martha, and Mitch Weiss, retellers. 2001. *Through the Grapevine: World Tales Kids Can Read and Tell*. Little Rock, AR: August House, pp. 71–72. 2 min. From G. R. Subramiah Pantaluh's *Folklore of the Telegus: A Collection of Forty-Two Highly Amusing and Instructive Tales* (1905).

The King's Child

When the king and queen remained childless, an old woman came to help them. She made suggestions one at a time, telling the king to clean up the environment, free the serfs, and declare peace. He followed her advice but still had no child of his own. He was, however, now known as the father of a prosperous kingdom!

Black, Judith, reteller. 1994. In *Ready-to-Tell Tales: Sure-Fire Stories from America's Favorite Storytellers*, edited by David Holt and Bill Mooney. Little Rock, AR: August House, pp. 35–37. 5 min.

The Miller's Daughter

This preface to the reworking of the Rumpelstiltskin story in novel form follows the traditional format of the tale until the final climax. The miller's daughter is so distraught with the enormity of getting the answer correct that she becomes speechless and thus loses her child. The novel tells of two boys, pursued by greedy villains, on a quest to save innocent lives and their meeting with a banished queen whose son was stolen eleven years earlier.

Schmidt, Gary D. 2001. *Straw into Gold.* New York: Clarion, pp. 1–6. 8 min.

The Mirror

The value of education is passed on through the story of a young man who refused to study. He was devastated when the young woman he wished to marry refused to take him seriously until he passed his examinations. She gave him a mirror to remind him of her. The mirror did much more than that—it became his talisman.

Livo, Norma J. 2001. *Story Medicine: Multicultural Tales of Healing and Transformation.* Englewood, CO: Libraries Unlimited, pp. 133–35. 4 min.

Moonchildren

This is a Norse explanation for the features seen on the face of the moon. Two children, Hyuki and Bil, are filling their pail at a spring filled with a liquid that inspires poetry and prophesy. When they accidentally spill the liquid, the Moon notices them and scoops them up to live with him. Poets still call to Bil the beautiful to sprinkle their lips with the magic spring water.

Hoffman, Mary, and Jane Ray. 1998. *Sun, Moon and Stars.* London: Orion. 2 min. From Snorn Sturlusson's "Deluding of Gylfi" in *The Prose Edda.* It was suggested by S. Baring-Gould in 1866 that Hyuki and Bil were the originals of the nursery rhyme characters Jack and Jill.

Music Charms the Pirates

Pirates overtake a famous musician sailing in his boat. He asks to be allowed to play his new composition before they kill him, and the pirates agree to listen. The music fills their hearts, and tears begin to flow form their eyes. The pirates decide to leave the musician in peace. The musician laughingly remembers the scorn he received growing up, constantly being told that music would never help him in a fight!

> Walker, Richard, reteller. 1998. *The Barefoot Book of Pirates*. New York: Barefoot Books, pp. 42–47. 6 min. Based on a brief description found in Margaret Read Mac-Donald's *Peace Tales* (1992).

Of Apples and Ants

A famous mathematician is asked to solve many problems, including the mystery of the ninety apples. A father gives his three daughters ninety apples to sell at the market. He gives the first sister fifty apples, the second sister thirty, and the third sister ten and then tells them that they must all ask the same price for the apples and return with the same amount of money. How can this be accomplished?

> Tahan, Malba. 1993. *The Man Who Counted: A Collection of Mathematical Adventures*, translated by Leslie Clark and Alastair Reid. New York: W. W. Norton, pp. 119–26. 9 min.

Sargon the Mighty: A Tale of Ancient Akkad

An abandoned baby is found floating down the river in a basket and is rescued by a gardener who raises him as his son. The goddess Ishtar was impressed with the growing young man and takes him under her wing. This ancient tale of the childhood of Sargon of Akkad, who ruled over the kingdom he founded, the land of Akkad (now part of Iraq) during the second millennium b.c.e., has been told in various forms and was found written on clay tablets from the eighth century b.c.e. (219).

> Sherman, Josepha. 1994. *Once upon a Galaxy: The Ancient Stories Behind Star Wars, Superman and Other Popular Fantasies*. Little Rock, AR: August House, pp. 57–58. 3 min. This ancient tale is closely related to the story of Moses in the bull rushes and is one of the forerunners of the Superman origin tale.

The Seventh Night of the Seventh Month

In this story from China, a pair of young lovers is rewarded for faithfully adhering to the virtues of loyalty and perseverance. Their eternal reward is the meeting of the constellations, Weaving Girl and Herding boy, on the seventh night of the seventh moon.

> Livo, Norma J. 2001. *Story Medicine: Multicultural Tales of Healing and Transformation*. Englewood, CO: Libraries Unlimited, pp. 107–110. 6 min. This story is a variation on the legend of the Blue Willow dinnerware pattern that played such a large role in the lives of early settlers in Western Canada and the United States.

Single-handed Success

A traditional Persian legend is told to demonstrate the material and the spiritual. Three wise men are each given two dinars and told to fill an entire room with the proceeds of this tiny sum. The first wise man fills the room with hay, the second with light from a candle, and the third spends no money at all but is clearly the winner. With what does he fill the room?

Tahan, Malba. 1993. *The Man Who Counted: A Collection of Mathematical Adventures*, translated by Leslie Clark and Alastair Reid. New York: W. W. Norton, pp. 207–209. 4 min.

The Singer and the Song

A young prince learns a drastic lesson when he assumes that a pure voice reflects a loyal heart.

Yolen, Jane. 2000. *Sister Emily's Lightship and Other Stories*. New York: TOR, pp. 123–24. 3 min. First published as liner notes for *Omayio*, a compact disk by Robin Adnan Anders.

The Story of the Didgeridoo

The story of the creation of the musical instrument that nonnative people call the didgeridoo and the Aboriginal people from the Gulf Country in Australia call a *yidiki*. After his death, Yidiki's spirit went into the hollow branch. Because there is a male spirit inside, the instrument can only be played by men.

Jones, Francis Firebrace, teller. 2001. In *Gadi Mirrabooka: Australian Aboriginal Tales from the Dreaming,* edited by Helen F. McKay. Englewood, CO: Libraries Unlimited, pp. 73–74. 2 min.

The Three Dolls

A king, who prides himself on his cleverness, boasts that he can solve any riddle set before him. But neither himself, the wise man, nor the fool can solve the riddle of the three dolls. It took a storyteller to do that!

Novak, David, reteller. 1994. In *Ready-to-Tell Tales: Sure-Fire Stories from America's Favorite Storytellers*, edited by David Holt and Bill Mooney. Little Rock, AR: August House, pp. 13–15. 5 min.

Three of a Kind

A retelling of the fable of the lion, the hyena, and the jackal and the division of the hunt demonstrates a division of three by three and a division of three by two, with no remainder.

Tahan, Malba. 1993. *The Man Who Counted: A Collection of Mathematical Adventures*, translated by Leslie Clark and Alastair Reid. New York: W. W. Norton, pp. 213–17. 6 min.

References

Barnette, Martha. (n.d.). Funwords Web site. Accessed at www.funwords.com/library/c.htm

Branston, Brian. 1974. *The Lost Gods of England*. New York: Oxford University Press.

Livo, Norma J., and Sandra A. Rietz. 1986. *Storytelling: Process and Practice*. Littleton, CO: Libraries Unlimited.

Swatridge, Colin. 1996. "A Pound of Flesh." *The Hindu* (December 31): 33, col. a.

Yolen, Jane. 1987. "Ethics and Storytelling. *National Storytelling Journal* 4(4): 5–7.

Zipes, Jack, ed. 2000. *The Oxford Companion to Fairy Tales: The Western Fairy Tale Tradition from Medieval to Modern*. Oxford: Oxford University Press.

Chapter 9

Sample Stories

I have included sample stories that have been tested for, and by, teens. Each tale is prefaced with a short introduction to place it in context and to give some background on the genesis of this particular retelling. Please feel free to adapt the tales that I have retold. The stories from other storytellers are also available for you to tell, but please note that their tales are copyrighted.

Tales of the Fantastic

Several of the stories in this section are based on historical figures, both in the distant and recent past. Others are adaptations of urban legends.

King Herla

I created this tale for a storytelling session on medieval tales several years ago. It is based on the story of this early British king by Walter Map (1140–1210), who was a clerk in the English royal household, an itinerant justice, a churchman, and a poet and writer. Map is usually credited with a portion of the work on Lancelot. Walter Map stated that the last time King Herla and his men were sighted was on the borders of Wales and Herefordshire, during the first year of the reign of Henry II (1154–89). They apparently appeared at noon, accompanied by wagons, beasts of burden, hawks, hounds, and people running along side of them. Armed bands came to meet and challenge them, but they did not reply on being attacked. They simply rose into the air and vanished. In later northern European folklore, Herla and his train became interpreted as a manifestation of the Wild Hunt, ghostly riders who ride through the sky on stormy evenings as an omen of evil. The Wild Hunt is also identified with the Saxon god Woden (the Norse Odin).

I like to believe that the small bloodhound in the tale is really a smooth fox terrier, just like the one I have at home. Just a coincidence, I am sure, but my smooth-fox terrier is known as Woden.

An additional note about King Herla is that his name is also associated with the word "Harlequin." The brightly clad buffoon, traditionally presented in a mask and diamond-shaped patterns, in the Italian commedia dell'arte may have originated from a mythical character known as Herlequin or Hellequin, who was the leader of a ghostly troop of horsemen who rode across the sky at night. The American Heritage Dictionary states that the etymology of Harlequin is "Obsolete French, from Old French "Herlequin," "Helleguin," a demon, perhaps from Middle English "Herleking," from Old English "Herla cyning," King Herla, a mythical figure identified with Woden" (www.bartleby.com/61/59/H0065900.html).

The old stories tell of an old king of Britain who dearly loved to hunt and ride through the forests of his realm. One day while riding, he met a strange red-bearded dwarf riding a goat. The dwarf greeted King Herla courteously. "I am the king of many kings, the lord of subjects without number. I have come to greet you, as you are a king like myself. I wish to join you at your upcoming wedding festivities and have you return the visit at my own wedding exactly one year from your own."

King Herla was surprised at the stranger's words, as he knew nothing of his upcoming wedding. "When you return to court this day," the stranger continued, "there will be ambassadors from the king of France waiting to offer you a bride."

The stranger disappeared, and Herla returned to his court to find the French ambassadors and the offer of marriage. King Herla agreed to the marriage for the maiden was both fair and richly dowered. Wedding plans were made and the days disappeared into a flurry of activity.

The day of the wedding arrived and a more handsome groom or a beautiful bride were difficult to imagine. The wedding party was just sitting down to a great feast when the dwarf king rode into the yard. He brought with him a bounty of gifts including goblets of crystal and rare gems and burnished gold, one for each guest as well as gifts of fine sweet meats. King Herla welcomed his guest and thanked him for the thoughtful gifts. When the feast was over, the dwarf king and his retinue departed and the newly wedded couple settled down to get to know one another better.

A year quickly passed, and it was now time for King Herla to be a wedding guest. He loaded a train of donkeys with an astonishing amount of fine gifts and set off for the home of the dwarf king. It was not very long until he and his men were met and lead through paths that were strange to them and far removed from any sign of human life. They followed their guides into a land of grey crags and barren wilderness, until they reached a cavern set in the steep and lowering face of a precipice. They entered the cavern, following the winding tunnels for a very long time until they burst forth into the light. There in the center of the cavern was a palace, a palace glowing as bright as the noonday sun from the myriad of candles and lamps in and around it.

King Herla arrived in time to celebrate the wedding feast of the dwarf king, a feast that lasted three days. At last it was time for Herla to return home. His host showered King Herla with gifts: horses, hounds, hawks and all those things related to the chase and to falconry. He then went with King Herla to the edge of the darkness that lay between his own realm and the wilderness.

"I have another gift for you," he told Herla. He handed him a bloodhound, one small enough to fit in the king's hand. "Let none of the company dismount from his horse and set foot to the ground, till the hound leaps out of the King's arm," was his final command.

Herla and his men soon rode out of the cave mouth back into the sunshine. There they met an ancient shepherd, a man so bent by the burden of his years that it weighed his shoulders down.

"How has my queen fared in my absence?" queried King Herla.

The shepherd stared at the king in bewilderment. "I scarcely understand your speech, my Lord, for you are a Briton and I am a Saxon. Yet I know that you ask for a queen whose name I have only heard in the old legends. The stories say that a queen so named was the wife of a king of this land who disappeared into a cliff one day and was seen no more on earth. But that was long ago, before we Saxons came to this land, and it is two hundred years since we have been here."

Herla was dumbfounded. It was but three days that he visited the dwarf king! What had happened? What did the shepherd mean? Before Herla could say anything in reply, several of his men leapt off their horses in astonishment. As they touched the ground, they crumbled into the dust.

Herla quickly commanded his remaining men to remain seated and to wait for the dog. But the dog did not leave King Herla's arms, not then nor to this day.

Some say that King Herla, his men and the dog are still endlessly wandering, roaming his former kingdom and never finding rest at all. Others know that the Wild Hunt is not something anyone should want to see.

Nicholas Flamel

This story is based on a discussion of Nicholas Flamel in Daniel Cohen's Raising the Dead *(New York: Dutton, 1997, 88–94). I used this text, along with additional research, on a recommendation of an eighth-grade student who asked me if I knew the story of Nicholas Flamel and the Philosopher's Stone.*

What connection does a fourteenth-century Parisian scribe have with people of today? Well, yes, we do scribble, but now we do so for ourselves, which was not the case in Nicholas Flamel's time. He made his living by writing letters and documents for the large portion of the population who could not write.

No, the connection is not with his occupation but with his dream about a book. A book that was to lead him on a merry dance for many years until he unlocked the secret. A book that has continued to lead others on that same dance, for Flamel never revealed the secret to anyone else. And the secret? Ah, the secret . . . it was the philosopher's stone and the power to transmute lead into gold!

You may be familiar with Flamel's name, after all he is featured in a related search for power and knowledge by a young boy named Harry, *Harry Potter and the Philosopher's Stone!*

For the most part, Flamel's life was quite ordinary. He earned enough to keep him and his wife Pernelle in comfort. They were happy with each other and with what life had to offer—happy, that is, until Flamel had a dream about a book. It was not an ordinary book; it was covered in symbols and a strange alphabet. Flamel could not quite make out what the book was about. As he reached out to bring it closer to him, an angel stopped him and spoke.

"Flamel," the angel announced, "This book will be of utmost importance to you. Look at it carefully so you will recognize it when you see it again. This book will be yours one day, but I must tell you, it is not one that you will be able to read or understand. One day, though, Flamel, you will be able to unlock the secret between its covers. Remember this book." The angel, the book, and the dream disappeared when Flamel awoke that morning, and some remnants of the dream lingered for a few days while he tried to make some sense of it. But soon, as many dreams do, it disappeared from his thoughts.

And then one day he remembered it vividly when the offer of a manuscript for sale brought it rushing back. It was the very same book of his dream: the color, the shape, and size. This book, like the one in his dream, was filled with alchemical symbols, and a text written in an unfamiliar language. There was only one paragraph that Flamel could understand, and that was because it was written in Latin. It proclaimed that the book was written by Abraham the Jew and was an alchemical text that contained the formula to turn lead into gold.

It truly was the book from his dream. He could not understand it, and neither could anyone else around him. For twenty-one years, Flamel attempted to decode the secrets of the book, but to no avail. Finally he made his way to Spain, to see if he could find a Jewish scholar who could decode the symbols for him. He spent an entire year visiting various Spanish synagogues, but still he could find no help. On his return journey to France, however, he met the man he had set out to find, a converted Jew, Maestro Canches. Canches immediately recognized the copies of the drawings Flamel showed him. They came from a long lost book, the *Ash Mezareph,* written by Rabbi Abraham. Although Canches died before he had a chance to see the actual book, he had given Flamel enough information for him to decode the secrets within it.

Now as Flamel studied the book with renewed passion, the secret was unlocked. He recorded in his journals that on January 7, 1382, he changed lead into pure silver. He then made the Great Elixir and, on April 25 of the same year, transmuted lead into pure gold! The angel had been correct. Flamel had indeed discovered the secret of the book.

You might think that Flamel used the formula to become a very rich man, but he did not. He was a man of science and a scholar, and it was not wealth that he sought but knowledge. He only transmuted the lead into gold twice more. With the wealth he gained, he endowed many churches, hospitals, and other charities around Paris. He then spent the rest of his life writing about alchemy, and yet, after his death, when people scoured his belongings for the secret, it could not be found. People are still searching, you know, searching for the secret of the book and the philosopher's stone.

Since the secret of transmutation is closely aligned to the search for the Elixir of Life in the minds of many people, rumors have circulated since Flamel's death in 1417 that neither he nor his wife were actually dead but living in exile elsewhere to avoid discovery. It was said that the Flamels did return to Paris to attend the opera in the mid–eighteenth century. They were recognized by other opera attendees from portrait drawings of the couple. It is also said that they had not aged at all in the four hundred years since their death!

The Phantom Ahead

by Catherine Crowley

This is a true story that tiptoes between reality and the supernatural without falling to either side. It is based on a 1945 account published in the London Times. Several variations of this motif have been developed since that incident. The tale is reprinted here with permission from the author, Catherine Crowley. Her rendition of the story first appeared in Storytelling World *(Crowley 1999). In her personal correspondence to me, she said, "I developed the story from a one-paragraph account of the event from a book about amazing facts. I never could find that book again. In Colorado, it is a winged grasshopper that alerts the engineer to the danger."*

Many bombs were dropped on London during World War II. This bombing was called the Blitzkrieg because *blitz* means lightning, and the bombs struck like lightning. People never knew who would get hurt or where it would happen. Families who lived in the city sent their children to the countryside so they would be safer—telling them they would be gone for just a little while because this war would soon be over. But a little while turned into a long while. Before long some children could not remember the color of their mother's eyes or if their father had a beard.

Finally the war was over. Trains began to take the children back to London. Big John, the engineer of one of the first trains to return, was thinking about how grand it was that all the children on board would soon be with their parents again. But something was bothering him. It was just a feeling that something wasn't quite right, and he couldn't get it out of his mind. He checked every gauge and dial in the locomotive as it sped through the countryside, but he could find nothing wrong. *He just had that feeling.* He watched the sun set and the hills glow as night began to wrap around them all. Big John flipped on the big light on the front of the train.

That was when he saw it on the tracks ahead! A man in a cape was standing right in the middle of the tracks. The man seemed to take his cape and raise it on either side of him like wings. Big John gasped as the hairs on his arms stood up.

Immediately he blew the whistle to scare the man off the tracks, but the figure never flinched, nor did he step away. Then he raised his cape again. Big John thought quickly, "It must be some poor fellow who was injured in the war and is having delusions. I'll blow the warning whistle once more, and if he doesn't move, I'll have to stop the train and get him off the tracks."

Once again the whistle blew long and loud. Those on the train wondered why. They knew they were still far out in the country. They pressed their noses to the windows and looked out into the night. As the train slowed down, some of the smaller children started to whimper.

Two conductors jumped off the train as it came to a stop. They began to run up to the locomotive, holding up their lamps for the engineer as he came to the edge of the cab.

"What's going on?" he yelled. Big John turned toward the tracks and pointed. "Bless my soul," they said together.

"Just go get him off the tracks!" Big John yelled. But both the conductors backed up and shook their heads. So Big John jumped down and said, "Follow me. I'll get him off!"

He grabbed one of the lanterns and walked toward the man, calling out as he went, "Say there! Get off the blooming tracks! Are you daft?" But the eerie figure just moved his cape up and down. The two conductors slowed in fear. They were barely moving, and they gulped as the man on the tracks shimmered with an eerie light. Even Big John slowed his pace. There was something so deathlike about the movements that it chilled them all. That man was not going to get off the tracks!

The two conductors were now far behind Big John, who thought of the train full of children. He felt the fear coming from all of them, and that made him angry! These children had been through so much—nothing should ever make them afraid again. The war was over, and the most evil forces in the world had been beaten back. By golly, *nothing* was going to stop these children from returning to their parents and living as families.

With new determination Big John walked faster toward the man on the tracks, yelling, "We didn't let Hitler stop us—or Mussolini—and whatever evil you are, you'll not stop us either!" But just then Big John tripped and fell hard, right into a huge deep hole!

The two conductors rushed forward and looked with amazement at the engineer lying at the bottom of a crater at least ten feet wide and several feet deep. As they held up their lanterns, they saw that the train tracks had been blown away! They forgot about the eerie figure and helped Big John out of the hole. As the three surveyed the damage, they realized that, unknown to anyone, one last bomb had exploded on the tracks! If the train had gone into the big hole where the tracks had been, people would have been hurt . . . or even killed. The men took their lanterns and headed back to the passengers to let them know that another way home would have to be found.

The two conductors went ahead as Big John paused and pulled out his handkerchief to wipe the dirt and sweat off his face. As he stretched his sore body, he looked up at the huge light on the front of the engine. To his surprise he saw a large butterfly stuck to the front of the light. As he walked closer, he could tell it was almost dead, but its wings were still slowly opening and closing. He noticed that as the light passed through the wings, it made a shadow on the tracks ahead. Big John was awed at how much that shadow looked like a man on the tracks, slowly raising and lowering his cape. He rushed back and explained to the passengers what had transpired.

The children did make it safely back to the city and to their parents. But neither Big John nor the children ever forgot that night, when not an eerie ghost but a butterfly saved the train!

Room for One More

My version of this contemporary legend began as a front-page story for a local weekly newspaper's Halloween edition several years ago. The editors had wanted a tale that "took place" in the immediate vicinity. When Dan Yashinsky put out a call for ghost stories, I decided to edit the story and take out the references to a specific community and let it be anyone's hometown. I have been telling this story for a long time, and, when revisiting it to place in this chapter, I was surprised at how much it had changed in the interim. This version of my story is reprinted from Yashinsky's (1997) book ghostwise: A Book of Midnight Stories.

My cousin Joseph was living alone on the top floor of a downtown high-rise apartment building when his friends invited him to spend the weekend at their newly renovated home in the country. He had never been there before but thought he could find it easily . . . even in the dark.

His friends gave him directions, telling him that it was easy to find. "Joseph, there are only two houses on the road, but ours you just can't miss. It's an old white three-story farmhouse—huge—with a wide gravel driveway that completely circles the house. We'll leave the lights on for you."

His friends knew Joseph well. His most dependable trait was that he was late for everything—he always had a good excuse, but he was always late. And this time was no exception. Although Joseph had carefully written down the directions, during the hectic time he had trying to leave his apartment, he left them by the telephone.

He did know the general direction of the farmhouse and its approximate location, however. Joseph's other well-known trait was his stubbornness. "How many roads can there possibly be around this town?" he thought to himself. After spending hours on the dark country roads, Joseph finally found his friends' house, and it was just as they had described it. It was large and luminous white in the moonlight. In the brightness of the yard lights, he could easily see the circular gravel driveway.

Although by this time it was very late, Joseph drove up to the house and parked his car by the front door. His friends opened the door sleepily. They told him to park his car around the back and to make himself at home in the guest bedroom on the third floor. They were going back to bed and would show him their house in the morning.

Joseph made his way to the bedroom, and after exploring the room and looking out the window that overlooked the driveway and the darkness beyond, he got ready for bed. It was late and he was certainly ready for a good sleep, but for some reason sleep just would not come. He lay there for a long time but finally decided to get something to read.

As he got out of bed he heard a noise outside the window, and looked out at the darkness. Although his friends had extinguished the outside lights, the moon gave just enough illumination for Joseph to see . . . an old-fashioned mail coach drawn by four coal-black horses on the gravel driveway below. Joseph stared in bewilderment, and then in amazement, as he watched a tall man descend from the coach. Not only was he as thin as a skeleton, but he had a long jagged scar that traveled down his face from just below his right eye, across the corner of his mouth, and disappeared into the high collar on the left side of his neck. As Joseph stared at him, the man raised a long bony finger, pointed straight at Joseph in the window and rasped, "There's room for one more."

Joseph pulled himself back from the window in horror. When he collected himself, he looked out again, but there was nothing to see. No coach. No horses. And no coachman.

"It's just a dream," Joseph thought to himself. "Or someone with a twisted sense of humor. But, just in case, I'll check the driveway in the morning. If it was truly a dream, there will be no signs of wheels and horses." Needless to say, Joseph could not fall asleep for the rest of the night. As the sun rose, he quietly made his way outside. The gravel showed no signs of horses and coach wheels.

"Just as I thought. It was a dream."

Disquieted from such a vivid experience, Joseph did not mention it to his friends. Instead, he pushed it to the back of his mind and enjoyed the day. That evening, however, it happened again. He could not sleep. He heard the noise outside his window and he went to it. The same coach, the same horses, and the same coachman were on the driveway below. He even heard the same warning! With his long finger pointing directly at Joseph in the upstairs window, the coachman repeated, "There's room for one more."

This time Joseph did not leave the window, but the coach and the horses and the coachman disappeared. They did not drive away; they just vanished from sight. "Enough," thought Joseph. He threw his belongings into his case, quietly but quickly went down the stairs and got into his car. He drove directly to his apartment, went upstairs, and fell asleep with no more conscious thought.

Joseph slept well and long. When he arose, it was mid-afternoon. His immediate hunger drove all thoughts of his adventure from his mind. "I need to eat something and, of course, there is no food here." He decided to go to his favorite eatery a few blocks away. As he waited for the elevator, he began to register the long passage of time. A Sunday afternoon was not usually a busy time of day in his apartment building. What was taking so long? He was so hungry!

When the elevator finally arrived, Joseph saw how packed it was. There was just enough space for him to squeeze in. As he began to step into the elevator, however, a long bony finger pointed at him. The words calling out to him propelled Joseph to follow the voice to gaze at the revolting face of the coach driver.

"There's room for one more," he dimly heard echoing through his mind.

Without thought, Joseph quickly hurled himself out of the elevator and stood there trembling as the doors closed in front of him and the elevator car proceeded to descend. Joseph stood there, silent and not moving for a long time, then started to quiver and shake. But it was not him vibrating, it was the building! The cables on the elevator car snapped, the car fell to the basement and everyone aboard was killed.

Joseph never stayed in his apartment again and has since moved to a walk-up, not too far from me.

A Twist in Life!

by Lawrence de Vos and Taryn de Vos

My son-in-law Lawrence developed this version of the urban legend to tell to teens at several group homes where we were telling stories in 2002. The members of the audiences were horrified by the tale, and each time it was told it started a lively discussion on responsibilities and consequences among the teens. My daughter helped him in turning his story from "one for the ears to one for the eyes."

Juliya had just received her high school diploma and was ecstatic because she was finally done. Thoughts of her future were running through her mind. She wanted to take a break before beginning university. Backpacking for a year in Europe sounded pretty good.

That evening, while Juliya was enjoying a celebratory dinner with her family, her parents inquired about her plans for the future. They were curious about which university she was planning on attending. Juliya had kept up her grades, so her parents had decided to pay for her to attend university.

Juliya's response shocked her parents; her plans of going to Europe were new and unwelcome news for them. After a lengthy and stressful discussion, her parents relented and decided to support her financially for the trip. They bought her a round trip ticket to Europe.

Juliya landed in Europe two weeks later. When she settled in Paris, she had no problems finding a place to live and a good job. In her spare time, Juliya traveled around Europe by train, seeing the sights. One morning while enjoying a latte in Italy, Juliya met Ernesto, a fellow traveler from France. It was love at first sight for both of them. The two lovers walked in the parks together, took trips to various museums, and enjoyed each other's company.

After a month, Juliya left the family she had been staying with and moved in with Ernesto. For months Juliya lived in bliss, surrounded by the French countryside and completely in love with her man.

Six months after arriving in Europe, Juliya realized she was pregnant. Having never talked to Ernesto about having children together, she felt confused and alone. For the first time in months, Juliya felt homesick. She decided that her best course of action would be to fly back home and talk to her parents about the child, and then she would return to her Ernesto. Ernesto sadly agreed to let her go.

137

The day Juliya was to fly home, Ernesto drove her to the airport. On the way they stopped at a florist shop. Ernesto came out of the store with a large white box and a silly grin on his face. He wouldn't let Juliya see what was in the box, telling her to be patient. At the airport Ernesto gave Juliya the white box, explaining that she could not open the box until she was at least 30,000 feet in the air. After a tearful goodbye Juliya boarded the plane. Although sad at the prospect of leaving Ernesto, Juliya was excited to see her parents, as well as to see what was in the box. As soon as they reached 30,000 feet Juliya opened the box. There were twelve black, long stem roses and a card.

Confused, Juliya, at first just stared at the card and then she bolted blindly to the bathroom screaming. A nearby stewardess, wondering what the commotion was all about, approached the seat Juliya had vacated. She looked at the seat, saw the roses and then blanched when she too read the card. In a beautifully written script she read, "WELCOME TO THE DISEASE THAT HAS NO CURE! WELCOME TO THE WORLD OF AIDS!"

Tales of the Folk

This trio of tales, two from Russia and one from Japan, come to us courtesy of three of my favorite storytellers. The trickster element in each story appeals to the young adult audience, as does the relationship between the two generations.

Old Frost and Young Frost

by Celia Barker Lottridge

This story is reprinted with permission from the author, who introduced it in Next Teller: A Book of Canadian Storytelling, *collected by Dan Yashinsky (1994) as follows: "This is a Lithuanian story, but all who live in cold countries will recognize Young Frost and his father. Take a walk in the snowy forest or down a windy city street and you will meet them. Do you know what to do? The poor woodcutter may teach you a few tricks" (15).*

You already know Old Frost. He's the one who sends shivers down your spine on cold winter days. He nips your toes and makes the tip of your nose turn red. Yes, you know Old Frost, but you may not know that he has a son called Young Frost. Like all sons, Young Frost likes to believe he is much more clever than his father. In fact, there are times when Young Frost thinks that he should be doing Old Frost's job himself.

On one such day Old Frost and Young Frost were sitting up in a tree in the snowy forest. As usual, Young Frost was begging for a chance to show how quickly he could make people sorry that they had ventured away from their cozy fires. He paused as a shiny sleigh pulled by a pair of well-fed horses passed beneath the tree. Inside the sleigh was a rich merchant, as well-fed as his horses and wrapped in furs. He wore fur-lined boots, a thick fur coat, a fur hat pulled well down over his ears, and he was covered by a shaggy fur blanket.

"Look at that one," said Young Frost. "He thinks he is safe from chills and shivers. Just give me a chance. I'll show you what I can do."

"All right," said his father, "go ahead. Show me."

Young Frost zipped down the tree and into the sleigh. He wound himself around the merchant's neck, looking for a little opening where he could slip in. And he found one, just at the back of the thick fur collar of the coat. Down he went, right down the man's back.

The man began to shiver. "Drive faster! Do you want me to freeze?" he shouted at the driver. He huddled into his coat, trying to wrap himself more tightly in the fur. But Young Frost had found his way into the wide tops of the boots and was busy nipping the man's toes. After that, he squeezed under the flaps of the fur hat and turned the merchant's ears bright red. Then he hung around, giving a shiver here and a nip there.

139

When the merchant reached home he was so cold he could hardly move. His wife had to sit him by the fire and feed him hot soup and tea.

Young Frost flew back to the tree, laughing. "Did you see what I did?" he said to Old Frost. "All those furs meant nothing to me. That man will not forget me soon."

Old Frost smiled his thin smile and the air crackled with cold.

"You did not do badly," he said, "not badly at all. Of course, that was an easy job." Young Frost was outraged but his father went on, "Sensible people know it takes more than furs to keep them warm when Frost is in the forest. Now if you really want to show what you can do, try him." And he pointed a long finger at a woodcutter who was guiding his sledge beneath the tree.

Young Frost looked down. He saw a man dressed in a thin, padded coat, ancient felt boots, worn leather mitts and a hat that had been furry long ago. His sledge was made of logs roughly nailed together and his horse was old and bony. He had an axe lying beside him. Anyone could see that he was going into the forest to cut wood.

"That one!" said Young Frost. "It will take no time to send him shivering home." But Old Frost just shook his head. "You can try," he said.

Young Frost slid down from the tree into the sledge. He quickly found a worn place in one of the woodcutter's felt boots and squeezed through it. He planned to give the woodcutter's toes a good nip but he had hardly begun before the man hopped out of the sledge and began running along beside his horse.

Young Frost was sure that he was going to be trampled inside the boot, but, just in time, he managed to find his way out of the hole. When he was safe he flew along behind the woodcutter, waiting for him to climb back into the sledge.

When he did, Young Frost was ready. He had spied a spot in the padded coat where a button was missing. He slid through the gap and settled down to send chills up the man's chest, around his neck, and down his back. But with the very first shiver of cold the man dropped the reins and began pounding his chest with his fists.

Young Frost had to hop to avoid getting thumped. No matter what cozy place he found, the pounding fists found him. It wasn't long before Young Frost was out in the fresh air, shaking his head.

"Never mind," he said to himself. "Just wait until he starts cutting wood. Then I'll get him." He had his eye on the woodcutter's ears where they stuck out below the flaps of his old fur hat.

The woodcutter stopped the horse in a little clearing among the trees and jumped out of the sledge with his axe in his hand, ready to get to work. Young Frost was ready too, but the woodcutter started chopping so furiously that wood chips flew everywhere. Young Frost couldn't get near those ears.

He was flying around thinking of how Old Frost would laugh, when the woodcutter paused to push his hat back from his forehead. "This work warms a man up," he remarked and, as if to prove it, he took off his mitts and threw them on the seat of the sledge. Then he gripped the axe and went back to his chopping.

Young Frost could not believe his luck. "I'll creep inside those mitts and make them so cold that he'll start to shiver as soon as he sticks his fingers in them. Then he'll forget all his wretched tricks and I'll have him." And Young Frost got busy inside the mitts.

The woodcutter went on chopping until he had filled the sledge with neatly cut logs. Then he put down his axe and picked up his mitts. They were frozen stiff. The man shook his head and slapped the mitts together. They rang like iron. He looked at the mitts and at his hands and shook his head again. "It's a terrible frost today," he said. " But I can cure it." He laid the mitts on the stump of a tree, picked up his axe and began to pound the mitts with the flat side of the axe.

He pounded until his mitts were soft again. Young Frost barely escaped with his life. He was so bruised and sore that he found a chink in the pile of logs and stayed there until the sledge passed under the tree where Old Frost waited. Even then he could barely fly up to the branch.

"What a terrible man!" he said to his father. "First he trampled me, then he thumped me, then he hit me with pieces of wood and finally he pounded me with an axe. You can have that job. I don't want it."

Old Frost laughed until the air glittered. "When you can outsmart a poor woodcutter who gets his living outdoors in all weathers, you'll be ready to take over my job," He said. "But, until then, it is the woodcutter and I who rule the winter forest."

King's Questions

by Cathy Spagnoli

This story is from Jasmine and Coconuts: South Indian Tales. *It is re-printed with permission from the publisher.*

Once, long ago, two men started to work for a king at the same pay, doing the same job—clearing the royal stables. Ten years later, one of them had become the king's closest advisor, while the other was still cleaning the stables. The stablehand grew jealous of the advisor, wondering why he had done so well. Finally, he could hid his curiosity no longer. He went before the king and bowed.

"Your majesty," he said. "If it please you, do tell me why I am still a stablehand while another who started work with me is now your trusted advisor."

As the king was about to answer, they heard the sounds of a cart's bells outside. "Go see who is making that sound!" ordered the king. The man rushed out and came back shortly, saying, "A newly married couple, sir."

"From where do they come?" asked the king. The man rushed outside again and then reported, "They live in Mysore, sir."

"And why are they traveling?" the king inquired. A bit tired, the man ran out again. In moments he returned and said, "They went to visit some relative, your highness."

"What type of work do they do?" the king then asked. Hoping that this would be the final question, the man stopped the couple once again. Soon he came back to report, "They are merchants, sir."

Just then, the king's advisor entered the palace room. The king turned to him and said, "Outside, I hear the bells of a cart. Go see who is making that sound." With a bow, the advisor left and was back in a moment.

"Your majesty," he said. "There are two people, newly married. They live in Mysore, but the woman's father is not well, so they went to visit him in Vellore. They are merchants who sell bangles in their small shop near a Siva Temple."

At that, the king turned to the stable hand. "Now, do you understand why you still work with the horses and he tells me how to rule the land? He found out more in one trip than you did in four!"

142

The Twelve Months

by Ruth Stotter

Reprinted with permission from the author, Ruth Stotter (1998), this Greek tale originally appeared in The Golden Axe and Other Folk Tales of Compassion and Greed. *The tale appears in many story collections and is a variant of Tale Type 480: Kind and Unkind girls. The heroes in these stories show compassion without calculating what they will gain by it. "They act as caregivers without being martyrs and in so doing demonstrate their worthiness for being helped themselves" (8). Tales of this tale type provide a blueprint for achieving individualization (a balanced selfhood) through an initiation rite, providing hope that no matter how abused and unhappy you may be, there is a chance that if you have integrity and help those less fortunate, you will survive (9).*

There was once a widow who had five children. The only work she could find was baking bread for a lady in her village who would not let her take even a crust of the bread home to feed her children. When she returned home, however, she would use the dough left on her hands to make gruel. This was all the family had to eat. Nonetheless, the children were plump as mullet while the children of the lady who employed the woman were thin as mackerels.

One day the village lady noticed this and told the widow she would have to wash her hands before she went home, as she was not to take any of the dough home with her. When the mother returned home that night, she could not make gruel, and there was nothing for her children to eat.

She said, "Children, I am going to go out to try and find food for you."

She walked and walked and was surprised to find a tent brightly lit with a twelve-candle candelabra. She saw twelve people inside, who said, "Good woman, come in and join us."

"Thank you, " she said, and she went inside. The people asked why she was wandering about, and she told them her plight.

Three of the young people, dressed in light clothing, asked, "Good woman, how do you get along with the months of the year? What do you think of March and April and May?"

"I like them," she said. "The earth is covered with flowers, the fruit trees blossom, the meadows are green. I am grateful for the spring of the year."

Then three people, dressed in even lighter clothing, asked, "And what do you think of June, July, and August?"

"Ah," she answered. "The warmth of summer ripens the fruit and grains. I am grateful for the summer months."

Now three people in light woolen clothing asked, "Tell us, good woman. What do you think of the months of September, October, and November?"

"Ah," she answered. "That is when we harvest the grains. The forest trees are red and orange and yellow. The full moon appears larger than ever. There is a briskness in the air. I look forward to the autumn months."

And now three people bundled up in warm clothing asked, "And what do you think of December, January, and February?"

The woman smiled. "I love the quietness of the winter months. At night snow glistens as if it were filled with tiny diamonds. And it is so cozy by our fire—we tell stories and sing songs. I love the winter months."

"Here good woman," the people said, "take this basket home to your children."

"Oh, thank you very much." And the widow ran home wondering what she would find in her basket. Imagine her surprise to find that it was filled with gold pieces! And so she was able to buy food for her children. She could even buy her own wheat so that she could make bread to sell in the village.

The lady in the village observed this and asked the widow how her good fortune had come about. When she heard about the gift from the people in the tent, she decided to go visit them. She found the tent, and the people saw her and said, "Greetings, mistress. How is it you have come to visit us?"

"I am very poor," she answered, "and I have come for your help."

"Perhaps we can help you," they said, "but first we would like to know if you have a favorite month."

"Oh," she answered, "I don't think I have a favorite month. The summer months are much too hot and the winter months too cold. Everything dies in the autumn, and it rains too much in the spring. Is there anything else you want to know?"

"No," they answered. "Here, take this basket."

Happily, the woman grabbed the basket and ran home. When she opened the basket, she found that it was filled with snakes, nothing but snakes. And that was the end of that woman.

Tales of Life

I have included sample stories that I have developed from family history, local history, and legendary history. Although the reader has permission, as long as they credit me as the author, to tell these stories as they are, I highly recommend using them as a prototype to developing stories from your own experiences, community, and family life.

The Legend of Mary Overie

The bare bones of this legend were found on a marker beside the river on the south side of the Thames River on a recent visit to London, and I could not resist bringing it home!

Before the construction of the London Bridge in the tenth century, John Overie was the ferryman who took travelers over the River Thames. Because there was a great deal of custom on both sides of the river, Mr. Overie became a very rich man. Yet although he did build an estate on the south side of the river, he was a miser and watched his money very carefully.

One day he devised a plan to save money. He decided to feign his death, believing his family and servants would fast out of respect for his passing. He would save food for a day. His plan fell immediately asunder when the servants, overjoyed with his death, proceeded to celebrate with a huge (and expensive) feast! The miser, so furious that he forgot himself, leapt out of the bed where he was lying in state, to the horror of his servants. One terrified maid picked up a broken oar and "thinking to kill the Devil at the first blow, actually struck out his brains."

His distraught daughter Mary immediately sent for her lover who, in haste to claim the inheritance, fell from his horse and broke his neck. Mary was more distressed than ever and devoted her entire fortune to founding a convent into which she retreated. This became the priory of St. Mary Overie (she became a saint because of her charity). During the reformation, it was called St. Mary Over the Rie (water) and is now known as Southwark Cathedral.

Mrs. Stone

This tale was developed from personal diaries and local histories to illuminate the trials and tribulations of pioneer settlers in Edmonton, Alberta, Canada. I have told it for more than a decade to visitors to Fort Edmonton Park, an open-air historical museum where I was a resident storyteller "bringing history alive through story." I was particularly struck by this incident that took place when the protagonist was fifteen, the average age of many of the members of my usual story listening audiences.

I usually preface the story with the tale of how I found the story in a diary and how the author of the diary referred to herself throughout by her married name, Mrs. Stone. I liked the story of the young girl's courage and the historical background of the community, but I could not tell a story about someone whom I could not identify. I did further research until I found out who Sally was before she became Mrs. Stone, and with that information in mind, I could tell part of her story. For the purpose of this book, I have changed the names of the characters involved.

I close the tale by reminding the listeners that the story took place not that long ago, and look how far we have traveled since then.

Sally arrived with her parents and brothers at the train station at South Edmonton in the early spring of 1893. Her father and oldest brother had come out the year before, claimed a homestead about six and a half miles from the tiny prairie town, and built a small house on the property. Bud, Sally's brother, stayed behind while their father returned east for the rest of the family. Sally's father was a surveyor, and it had always been his dream to be a rancher; he could hardly wait until he could fulfill his dream.

They finally arrived, but, as they reached the tiny house, they soon realized that Bud had not expected them to arrive so early in the year. The house had been used as a granary, and there was no room for the family to set up housekeeping until it had been emptied. Their first night in their new home was spent in the attic; it was cold, but it was home.

About three weeks after they arrived, all their cows disappeared from sight. At that time, there were no fences, and people did not mind if their livestock wandered about. But Sally's father wanted his cows where he could see them.

"Boys, get on the horses and bring those cows back home."

Sally's brothers got on the horses and went looking for the cattle, leaving Sally and their parents on the homestead. Some time later, Sally's father thought he could see something moving on the horizon.

"I think those may be my cows. Sally, can you bring me my telescope?"

"I know where it is, father. I will get it." All of his surveying equipment was stored in the attic and Sally knew that the telescope was just inside an opening that had been cut in the outside wall of the attic. In order to get it, she had to climb up a ladder that had been set against the wall. While she was reaching inside for the telescope, her father picked up a double-barrel shotgun that had a quirky trigger. He had told his children not to load the gun because he had not had time to check it out, so when he pulled back the trigger to see what was wrong with it, he assumed that the gun was empty. He assumed wrong! The barrel was filled with duck shot and it went right through Sally's ankle as she stood on the ladder.

At first she did not realize that she had been shot, but as soon as she tried to put weight on her ankle to descend the ladder, she began to fall. Her horrified father, throwing the gun down, ran and caught her, screaming for his wife to come to help.

Since the boys had taken all the horses and there was no phone service out in the country, Sally's father started to run the six and a half miles into town. He ran into his eldest son about half way there.

"Bud, turn the horse around and ride back into town. Get a buggy and bring the doctor back home. There has been a terrible accident, your sister is hurt bad."

Bud turned the horse back to town, rented a buggy, it was a sulky,[1] a one-seater, but it was the only thing that he could get, and then got the doctor. The doctor was a drunk, and at this particular time he could hardly stand. But he was the only doctor who practiced in the town. Bud loaded the doctor into the sulky and held him there all the way home.

When they got to the homestead, the doctor had a surprise: somewhere, somehow, he had lost his medical bag and had nothing with him that could help Sally.

"Bud, get back on that horse, go into town and see if you can phone old Doc. Milson from across the river."

Bud rode back the six and a half miles to town, got hold of a telephone and phoned Doc. Milson from the town across the river. Now during that time there was no bridge crossing the river and joining the two frontier communities. There was a ferry that took travelers across, but it only ran in the summer months. This was spring break up. The river was running too fast, with the ice floes tearing at the shore and anything that was in its path, for anyone to cross it at all. Bud waited on one side of the river, the doctor on the other, for an entire day until the doctor could make it safely across. They hurried to the homestead and by the time they got there, the first doctor was sober. The two doctors looked at Sally's ankle and decided that there was only one thing they could suggest. The foot would have to be cut off!

"No, you cannot do this. I was born with two feet and that is how I will die!"

And although Sally was only fifteen, and only a girl, the two men listened to her. They did not cut off her foot, but there was nothing much that they could do for her. They left her in the care of her mother who put a poultice[2] on her foot every few hours. Her mother tried everything she could think of—lifting her foot, moving it this way and that, and finally, after two months in bed, Sally could hobble around the homestead on homemade crutches that her father made for her.

At the age of nineteen, Sally married Mr. Stone, a fur trader from up north. Because she wanted to look fine on her wedding day, Sally took a razor blade, opened up the scar tissue on her ankle and scraped out the black duck shot that had gathered there. Every couple of years, she had to reopen the scar tissue to scrape out the remaining duck shot.

Sally married Mr. Stone, moved up north, and had many more adventures. When she died, she died quite happily, with both her feet still on!

Notes

1. A light, two-wheeled, one-horse vehicle for one person, especially used in trotting races.

2. A soft mass of bread, bran, and kaolin (fine clay), usually made in boiling water and spread on muslin or other material and applied to sore or inflamed part. Sally's mother used flaxseed.

O-Per-Rue

While I was growing up I heard numerous family stories about the Edenbridge Colony, a Jewish colony, in the province of Saskatchewan. My grandparents lived in proximity of the colony and participated in the high holidays and other traditional celebrations. But because of the distance between their homestead and the colony, they were isolated from other Jewish families during most of the year. My mother moved away from the area when she was sixteen, and her parents went with her. Her first visit back to the homestead was in 1992. Their house, which my grandfather had built, had been moved off the original site but not destroyed. Rather, it had been used as a granary. My mother found it, and to her amazement, she discovered that the house had "shrunk" during the interim. But the stories remained the same!

"O-per-rue!" Esther would shout and Millie would convulse with laughter. Everyone else around the table would look at the two women and demand an explanation. When none was forthcoming, the two women would explode in laughter once again, and everyone would get angry.

"What does it mean?" everyone would insist. Again, the only answer they received was laughter.

And the truth of the matter was that the word did not mean anything. It was a word that Esther and Millie made up and used to help them handle the stress of dealing with their mother-in-law who had very little use for them at all.

Two green city girls, in the early 1920s, who did not know how to cook, clean, garden, or farm! How could they possibly be good wives for her sons? Not only that—Esther and Millie were sisters. Two sisters marrying two brothers and living on the same farm as their in-laws, although in separate households. The mother-in-law would lose her control over both sons!

"O-per-rue!" Esther and Millie would shout as they discovered that the recipe their mother-in-law gave them lacked an essential ingredient and that their effort could not possibly taste as good as that of their mother-in-law.

"O-per-rue!" they would cackle as Esther carried the freshly baked bread out to the chickens, the only creatures that would attempt to eat it.

"O-per-rue!" they would say to each other as their mother-in-law chased their husbands out of the kitchen where they had been helping to knead the bread dough.

"O-per-rue!" they would whisper as once again their husbands refused to stand up to their mother to defend their wives.

"O-per-rue! O-per-rue! O-per-rue!"

The mother-in-law should have been sympathetic. Like Esther and Millie, she, too, had an important relationship with her own sister. She also moved to the Jewish colony of Edenbridge, Saskatchewan, to be near her sister. She even had a close relationship with her own daughter who still lived at home. Perhaps that was part of the problem. Although she did not need the companionship of these two foreign daughter-in-laws, she resented their closeness. Esther and Millie were Jewish, true, but from England, not from Russia, and they could speak the language of the wider community and men folk. Their mother-in-law never learned to speak English or understand it at all.

The mother-in-law problem might not have been so huge if Esther would not have followed her sister's footsteps. It was Esther who caused the problem—not even Esther, the person, but Esther, the name! You see, Esther was also the mother-in-law's name. The concern arose because of a Jewish tradition that children, and grandchildren, would be named after a relative that lived a long and healthy life. The older Esther knew that her grandchildren would never be named for her if one of her sons married an Esther. And if the sister of Esther also was married to one of her sons, not one of her grandchildren would carry her name. This was a very important issue in her life. So important, as a matter of fact, that she had erected barriers to Esther's wedding for several years before it actually took place.

"O-per-rue!"

The two sisters took refuge in their relationship with each other and, while making it stronger by facing a common enemy, also drove a wider wedge into the problem. They did not need to get along with their mother-in-law and soon gave up the attempt. The arrival of grandchildren did not soften their mother-in-law's heart, nor did the fact that both women became respected for their productive garden plots and, eventually, even for their cooking. She never forgave them for standing up to her and erecting their own protective barriers and coping strategies.

She was right about the thing that bothered her the most. Both her daughter-in-laws have great-granddaughters named Esther; and neither of these Esthers are named after her. Both Esther's and Millie's great-granddaughters are named after my grandmother, Esther, who taught me early in life to stand up for myself and for what I believe in. It was a lesson she passed to her daughter and from her to me. Strong women run in our family and if you don't believe me, "O-per-rue"!

Taryn's Jump

by Gail de Vos and Taryn de Vos

Taryn and I wrote "Taryn's Jump" for this chapter years after the actual jumping competition. The original story was never captured in print, and I fear the angst that drove the tale is no longer apparent. When we finished writing it, however, we read it to her husband, Lawrence, who had never heard the incident before. His horror reminded us, once again, that love is not easy and that many compromises must be made, regardless of the relationship—husband and wife, parent and child.

My mother was petrified of water, as a result I am afraid of swimming and any form of water sport. When I became a mother, I decided that my children would not be limited by my fears. I even took swimming lessons with them when they were babies.

So when my daughter Taryn wanted to take horse-riding lessons, I did not dissuade her, even though the thought of my little girl on a horse terrified me. I thought she was so vulnerable on the back of a horse. After many years of Taryn taking lessons, I thought I was ready to watch her in a schooling show.

She was riding a "green horse" named Olga that she had used for lessons that year. This was Olga's first show. Taryn was really excited about this particular day as she wanted to show off Olga to us and the other spectators. Olga was curious but calm until she was warming up over the jumps. She noticed the crowd and began to get nervous. Nonetheless, she still responded to Taryn's cues.

The first few jumps of the course were against the far wall opposite the crowd. Olga took them gracefully, but when she came around the corner, the noise from the spectators distracted her. Although she made it over the first jump in the line, she stopped dead at the second. It was pink! Olga always had a problem with pink jumps, regardless of the fact that horses are presumed to be color blind.

Although Olga stopped dead; Taryn did not! She, not so gracefully, flew over Olga's left shoulder and did a head plant into the jump standard. Taryn slid to the ground, sat up, and insisted that she was fine. When she got back on the horse to jump once more, I immediately left the arena. There was a small spectators' room adjacent to the ring, and I huddled there until I heard her helmeted head hit the standard the second time. I was at the window, tears running down my face, searching the ground to make sure she was all right. She was, but she was also getting back on the horse! By this time, my husband had found me and was sheltering me from the ring. The jump was lowered, and Taryn and Olga tried the third time. Olga chipped, coming right to the jump, and then refused it. Taryn went straight over Olga, did a full sommersault, and landed on her bottom. The entire arena was then cleared of spectators and other horses. The people crowded into the small room where my husband was trying to comfort me. The riding instructor came in to reassure me that Olga was not the type of horse to stampede or step on a fallen rider. This did not console me because up until then I had only been worried about Taryn's head.

Taryn got on the horse again, not even noticing the empty arena. Her sole focus was to get Olga to make that jump so that she would not learn to refuse them in the future. My sole focus was not to insist that Taryn get off the horse because I knew this was something she had to do.

The jump was lowered to just a pole on the ground. The crowd gathered at the window, uncomfortable with the emotional outpouring coming from the corner where I stood. This time I could not see anything, but I did hear the applause when Olga took not only that jump, but the next one in line as well. Taryn stayed on the horse, and Olga completed the course before Taryn would willingly get off her.

When the show resumed, Taryn removed Olga from the arena, untacked her, and cooled her off. I gathered my composure and went and sat in the arena again to watch the other riders. I was horrified when Taryn came back into the arena, approached another horse, and rode the course again. It was a clean round until the last fence, when her new mount cantered right past the jump. I was not the only spectator to breathe a sigh of relief when that ride was over.

The judges were so impressed with Taryn's accomplishments, they awarded her a fourth-place ribbon even though a refusal is an immediate disqualification at a show.

Taryn was extremely buoyant with the fact that she and Olga had completed the course. She was also pleased with her fourth-place ribbon. I, on the other hand, disappeared into a hot bubble bath and a good book for the rest of the evening.

Taryn has continued to ride (and fall off) horses, but I have never watched her ride again. I never discouraged her from riding, but I just could not face my own fears.

Tales of the Spirit

The two stories in this section come from diverse origins. One is an excerpt from a fantasy novel, written by an author who clearly understands the oral tradition and the world of folklore. The second, captured by a storyteller and based on a traditional Native tale for which he has permission to set down in print, reflects the world of the spirit in another guise.

Gest and Mara

by Midori Snyder

Reprinted with permission from the author (Snyder 1987). This excerpt is told within the context of the novel itself. A few years ago, with permission from Midori Snyder, I told this story at the wedding of my friends. It was an unqualified success. As we sat in a large tent by the edge of the lake, the tears on the faces of the audience was reflected by the storm outside. I braided hair from my daughter's horse to give to the bride and groom after the story was told. Although I do have long flowing hair myself, there is no way it could be described as the color of flax.

Once in the ancient days, there lived a man named Gest and a woman named Mara. They were much in love and lived together happily. They had a neat stone house that looked down at the edge of the sea. Gest was a large man, tall and big, with a chest like the prow of a boat, black haired and black eyed. He was a fisherman and every day he rode the waves in his boat, traveling the gray-green sea to call the shoals of fish into his nets. Mara was a small woman, fingers slender as thread, and long fine hair the color of flax. She was a weaver and knew the secret craft of twisting life into the threads. Gest built their stone house with windows facing the sea that Mara might be inspired by the shifting colors of the waters. She wove them into her tapestries: silver fishes that leaped in the blue waves and white birds that dived into patterns of foam. You could hear her working, the steady pounding of the treadles, while Gest sang to its rhythm and repaired his nets for the next day's catch.

One day while Gest was at sea, Mara looked from her loom and saw the colors of the day changing; dark, heavy clouds matted the sky and turned the sea to an angry slate. She feared for Gest, afraid he'd not return home before the storm unleashed itself. She left her loom and went to wait by the shore. She stared out across the horizon hoping for a sight of his boat. The rain began to fall and the wind pushed the waves higher on the shore to lash the rocks. Still she waited in the driving rain, clutching her shawl tighter about her head. And then she saw his boat. Its mainsail was torn and it limped toward shore like an injured bird. She watched as Gest strove to keep the boat abreast of the growing waves. And then she saw the one terrible wave that turned the little boat like a top and crashed over its prow, breaking the mast and flinging Gest into the sea. "Gest!" she screamed, but the wind tore away her word. She waded into the sea, desperate to reach him, but her wet skirts weighed her down and the waves drove her to shore again. She saw his head bobbing in the water, his arms trying to keep himself afloat.

There was nowhere to turn for help. If she went to the village, it would be too late. She had to find a way to save him herself. She must use the gifts she had. She pulled three strands of her flax-colored hair and wove them into a braid. She called upon her weaver's gift to give the strand a life. Tying a key to one end, she cast it into the sea and charged it to find Gest. She held the other end wrapped tight around her hand. The frail rope of hair grew and stretched across the open sea. When it found Gest, floundering, his head near under the water, it wrapped itself around his waist. Mara felt the tug and began, slowly, to haul Gest ashore. As she worked, pulling his weight hand over hand, she thought only of their shared love. Into the string she gave every joy, every hardship, and every act of love that she had shared with Gest. The fragile rope held like a thread of iron, for such was the strength of Mara's love for Gest, and his for her. At last she pulled him into the shallow waters. Helping him to stand, she gave him her shoulder for support and stumbled home in the rain.

Mara's thread of hair was the first soulstring. Since that time, there is always the gifting of a soulstring at a wedding. It reminds us of the power of love, and as the love between a husband and wife deepens, so is the power of the soulstring strengthened.

Why All Tongues Are Red

by Dan Yashinsky

Scorch was greedy. He owned all the fire in the world, and he kept it all to himself. He made his fire blaze high in his cave, staring at the bright flames and the dancing shadows. He had one eye, and it was red.

The world was cold in those days, cold and quiet. It was cold because Scorch guarded his fire well. In the long winter of the early world, nobody but Scorch had the warmth of the fire. And it was quiet, too, because in those days human beings did not have tongues. We used the language of hands and the language of pictures to talk in those days.

A hunter had once ventured near Scorch's cave. He'd seen the fire, felt its warmth, marveled at its brightness. But the fire ogre had spotted him with his bright vermilion eye and thrown a burning coal at him. Scorch wounded the hunter, who barely managed to escape. By the time he staggered back to his people, the hunter was nearly dead. Before he died, he used the language of pictures and the language of his hands to tell what he had seen. For fire, he made a pile of sumac twigs, bright red.

Then he drew a picture of Scorch, and put a red berry in the middle of his head to show the one glaring eye. He held his hands over the sumac twigs to show that they were warm. He pointed at the drawing and drew his finger across his throat to show high danger. His wife and his daughter and son held him close, but the wound was too deep.

The people had gathered around the hunter and his grieving family. They looked at these strange drawings and shook their heads. They looked at each other. They shrugged their shoulders. Nobody's hands said anything—people were confused and frightened.

The hunter's daughter was heartbroken. She loved her father, and now he was gone. She kept staring at the sumac twigs and wondering what her father had seen deep in the forest. Red was her favourite colour. She'd dyed her moccasins bright red, and she loved cardinals. She was curious about this strange red force her father had drawn. She knew how cold her mother was in the long winter. She knew her little brother shivered from the cold. She decided to see the sumac-coloured thing for herself.

One day her mother went out to pick berries, and the girl was babysitting her little brother. She decided to take a walk in the forest. Usually the little boy napped for a long time, and she figured he'd sleep while she explored. She left him sleeping in their tent and began to walk into the forest looking for clues. She went in the direction her father had pointed before he died.

She walked a long ways.

She walked until she forgot what time it was.

Meanwhile, back at their tent the little boy woke up. He looked around for his sister. She wasn't there. He couldn't call out for her so he climbed out of bed and started to look for her. He saw the trail leading into the forest, and he started to follow it. Like all children back then, he was a good trail-follower. But somewhere deep in the forest he lost her trail.

She had been wandering a long time when all of a sudden she smelled smoke. It was a new smell to her. It was the smoke from Scorch's private fire. She followed it until she came to a clearing in front of a cave. She crouched in the bushes and watched. There at the entrance of the cave was the most beautiful thing she'd ever seen. Orange and scarlet flames leapt up, sparks cracked up into the air, and the smoke rose grey. Then Scorch appeared. He hunched out of the cave and crouched beside the fire. He was huge and ugly and his one red eye flashed suspiciously around the clearing. She wanted to run away, but she couldn't take her eyes away from the fire. Scorch tossed some dry logs on the fire, and it crackled and burned and looked even lovelier.

Just then she heard the sound of footsteps. Her little brother stumbled out of the bushes, directly in front of Scorch's cave. He had been wandering in the forest looking for his big sister. She couldn't call out a warning—she had no tongue to call with—and she watched with horror as the fire ogre reached out from the cave, curled his claws around the little boy and pulled him inside.

The girl didn't know what to do. Her mother might be picking berries nearby, but she couldn't yell for help. If she ran for the village it might be too late to save the little boy. She decided to fight the ogre all by herself.

She reached down and picked up a rock. Then she stamped her foot to draw his attention. When Scorch turned to see what made the noise, the girl used all her strength to hurl the rock straight at his one glaring eye. Scorch saw her, reached into the fire and picked out a glowing coal. He threw it and it raced towards the girl. He threw it with deadly aim. Her mouth was open and the burning coal flew in. It scalded her mouth, landed deep in her throat and took root there. Scorch's ember turned into the world's first tongue, and when it did, she cried out in pain, and that was the first sound human beings ever made with their voices. Babies have been making that sound ever since, as soon as they're born.

The ogre's coal hit her, but her aim was true. The rock she threw knocked out the ogre's one eye. Blinded, he stumbled and pitched forward and landed in his own fire. His body blazed up like dry cedar twigs, sizzling and scorching in the flames, and there was a great explosion.

She ran past the fire into the cave, and found her little brother. He opened his mouth and started talking - for everybody had received their tongues at the same moment the coal stuck in her throat - and said: "I was really really scared but I knew you'd find me because you're my big sister and why did you leave me all by myself and isn't fire beautiful and wasn't that one-eyed monster ugly and now we won't be cold anymore and I wish Daddy could have seen you clobber him and he was wrong to keep fire all to himself and there's Mama coming through the woods."

Their mother had heard the huge explosion and come running. She hugged her two children and said, "Are you alright?" That's still the first thing mothers - and fathers - say when they find their kids, before getting mad at them for being lost in the first place.

"Yes, mama," said the girl. "We're fine." And she stuck her thumb up to show they were. Even though she could talk now, she still liked to speak with her hands. "And look at the fire, mama. Isn't it lovely? We won't be cold anymore. It was wrong for that mean one to keep it all to himself. Now we can share fire with everyone who needs it."

"And can we have a snack when we get home because I'm starving and I think I have the best big sister in the whole world and that bad guy was really ugly and I think I'm going to like talking," said the little boy.

Little brothers—and sisters—have been doing a lot of talking ever since.

And so the girl, her mother, and her brother shared their fire with everybody in the village, and the tribe, and the whole early world. Since that day human beings have used fire to stay warm, cook soup, bake bread, harden pottery, melt metal, make toast, launch rockets, dry wet socks, burn things down, gather people into storytelling circles, and kindle light.

Since the coal landed in the girl's mouth, all human beings have had tongues, and all tongues are red, from the colour of the fire they came from. Like fire, our tongues can be used to bring light or tell lies, to sing or to curse, to cry freedom or speak hate. Best of all, we use our good, red tongues to tell stories.

Tales of Laughter

The origins of the three tales in this section are basically jokes and tall tales that have culled from the world of folklore and personalized by the retellers. Bring these tales home as contemporary tales or adapt them, as Merle does, to fit into a specific theme.

The Final Exam

This story was traveling the Internet for several years, and many people have retold it as a true story. A similar variant was collected and published by Nina Jaffe and Steve Zeitlin in The Cow of No Color: Riddle Stories and Justice Tales from Around the World *(1998) as "The Test" (134–36).*

Lawrence and Peter decided one evening that they should celebrate Peter's birthday instead of preparing for their final history exam the next day. Lawrence threw a big party for him, and they and their friends partied long into the night. They decided to have a quick hour nap and then get up and cram for the history exam. It was a procedure they had perfected throughout their university experience.

But this time they forgot to set the alarm clock and both overslept, missing the nine o'clock exam start.

"Time for plan B!" exclaimed Lawrence, and the two of them sat down over breakfast to decide what shape that plan should take. Soon they came up with a foolproof plan.

Running into the exam room, they met with their professor just as the examination was finishing. "Professor Jones, Professor Jones!" they panted in unison. "We have just had a terrible time getting here. We were away visiting Peter's old aunt yesterday and drove back last night. In the middle of the night, we had a flat tire. There was no spare tire in the car, and Lawrence's cell phone wasn't working. We had to walk for an hour to find a phone—that stretch of highway is so deserted. It took three hours before the tow truck could get to us and tow us back into town. And we raced over here as fast as we could. Professor Jones, what can we do? This exam is worth 65 percent of our final mark!"

Both Peter and Lawrence were surprised when Professor Jones was so accommodating. "Just come back tomorrow, and I will give you a makeup exam."

The students were jubilant. "It worked!" They both returned home to study and prepare for the exam the next day. Once again they crammed all night and got no sleep but at 9 o'clock the next morning, they were ready to write the exam.

"I can't be here to monitor you," Professor Jones told them, "I will just put you in separate rooms. Please bring the completed exam to the office as soon as you are done." He gave them their exam sheets and their examination booklets and closed the doors of the two rooms.

Both Lawrence and Peter looked disbelievingly at the one and only question on the exam. "Which tire?"

The King and His Jester

by Merle Harris

This is a brief tale from Jewish folklore, adapted one day when Merle was asked on radio to tell a story that involved patchwork and quilting.

Back in the mists of time, when life was very different from today, kings vied with one another for the ability to say their court jester provided the finest entertainment. One king employed a very young court jester who was a brilliant juggler and entertainer but, more than anything else, the jester had a gift of the gab and told the most wonderful stories. After making subtle enquiries during the day, he would make up songs and stories about the king's guests and weave them into his evening's entertainment. The stories had everyone in stitches and his own monarch laughed loudest and longest.

The jester's fame spread. People who heard and saw him exclaimed about his brilliance, and the king basked in the glory of having the best court jester in the country.

The king and queen, who entertained constantly, never wore the same outfit more than once. There was an army of seamstresses and tailors kept busy designing and making gowns and robes. The jester would slip in and entertain them, while at the same time helping himself to pieces of velvet, taffeta, brocade, silk, satin and other rich fabrics. Over many months he fashioned a floor length cape with pockets large enough to hold the tools of his trade.

The king had decided to have a tournament of sorts—a lavish evening of feasting interspersed with performances by the attending king's court jesters to see which was the finest. The evening was well on its way. The food was delicious and plenty and the entertainment had been brilliant. The time came for the resident jester to perform.

The king caught his breath when the jester strode into the banquet hall dressed in a magnificent cloak. He had never seen the costume before; it was a patchwork kaleidoscope of colors and textures, trimmed top and bottom with ermine.

The jester's performance was stunning—he balanced wine glasses on his nose, pulled roses from the ladies ears, and performed the most amazing juggling and acrobatic feats, all the while his cloak undulating around him.

In between his acrobatics and magic he was spinning the cleverest of stories and the entire audience was fully engaged. The king and queen were enjoying themselves tremendously when they suddenly realized that their jester was very subtly insulting them and some of their guests.

The stories revolved around the patches in his cloak and incidents when they had been wearing certain outfits. The king was outraged and stood up shouting "Enough! Not another word, you have insulted our guests enough! Because of your insolence I hereby order you to die!"

There was a sudden silence in the room broken by the jester, "You order me to die because I am doing what you expect me to do? Making fun of people. That is what you pay me to do? I do not understand you."

"This time you have gone too far, your stories may have been cleverly disguised by they were insulting and harmful."

"Your majesty this is too much to take in—please, I beg of you, change your mind. Have I not entertained you and your guests for many years? Have I not brought much goodwill to your court?"

The king calmed down slightly, thinking carefully and replied, "Indeed you have been a fine court jester and one I hate to lose. However, I will not take back the death order, but to show you that I am a fair king, I will give you two days to decide how you choose to die. Take him down to the dungeons."

The jester was put in chains and taken away and the guests vanished quickly.

Family and friends asked permission to visit the jester and to help him make his decision, but the jester refused to see anyone, saying he had got himself into this problem and he alone could make the decision.

The two days passed and the jester was brought before his king. The huge throne room was filled to overflowing with many people who wanted to be there to hear the jester's choice.

"Jester," said the king, "today is a painful day for me, you have given me so much pleasure over the years. Have you made your decision?"

"Indeed, I have. Before I tell you how I want to die, do I have your promise that you will carry out my decision."

"You have my word," replied the king. "How do you choose to die?"

"Oh, your majesty, all things considered, I choose to die of old age."

There was silence and the king threw back his head and roared with laughter. "Jester, your decision is accepted, and your position is open just as long as you never again insult a soul."

The court jester spent many more years entertaining the king's guests and eventually died as he had chosen, from old age.

My Mother's Pets

This is the story I lovingly refer to as my mother's story because I developed it for a Mother's Day program where I knew she would be in the audience. I caution tellers about doing something like this with their parents as victims—I mean characters—unless they have a very good relationship with them beforehand.

When my mother was a young girl living on the farm in the middle of the prairie, she desperately wanted to have a pet, an animal she could call her own. But her parents were practical people and because money was tight, they felt that any animal on a farm should be a working animal and not a pet.

Still, my mother persevered and kept after them for a pet. My mother was, and still is, a very effective whiner but still they said no. Then one day, things changed for the better. My mother spied a neighbor walking down the road carrying a large pail of water. And in the water, there was a young white fish.

"Please may I have it for my pet?"

"If you parents agree, then yes, it can be yours."

My mother ran home and pleaded with her parents. "I promise it won't be any trouble, it won't cost anything. I'll feed it with bugs and flies and it can live in the rain barrel. Please!"

This time they said yes, so my mother brought the white fish home, dumped it into the rain barrel and gave it a name. She called it Spike. And she did take good care of Spike for the first little while. She and her brothers and sister would catch flies and bugs and drop them into the water for Spike to eat. Once a week, my mother would clean the water in the rain barrel, for if you know anything about fish, then you know they are pretty dirty. At first this was not a problem. Mom would empty Spike into a pail of water and then clean the barrel before refilling it. But if you know anything about white fish, you know that they grow to a pretty large size and soon it wasn't fun taking care of Spike. It was work. And my mother, well, she was, and still is, pretty lazy and work was not what she was interested in doing.

She thought there must be another way to handle the situation that would not be so labor intensive. She thought and she thought and she thought again. And then she had an idea. She would train Spike to live outside of the water; that way, she would never have to clean the barrel again!

So the next morning, mom took Spike out of the barrel and put him in the wet grass for about five minutes. The next day, it was for a bit longer, and each day she added to the time that Spike spent outside of the barrel. Soon, it was an hour, then a full afternoon, and finally, Spike only had to be put in the water at night.

One night, however, mom forgot to put Spike back in the water. Horrified, she ran out the next morning to find—Spike—and he was just fine. Mom had done it, she had trained Spike to live outside of the water and now he was like a regular type of pet. He followed her around like a dog, although he wriggled like a snake. He even went to school with her. You have heard, I presume, of Mary and her little Lamb? Well, this was Lillian and Spike! The other kids loved it. They would play with Spike before school and at recess and then Spike would follow mom back home again when the school day was over.

One day, while they were at school, there was a terrible windstorm. The teacher would not let the students outside at all, not even my mom to check on Spike. When the wind finally calmed down, mom rushed outside to check on Spike and there he was—perfectly fine! Spike was such a smart fish.

They started walking home and mom was noticing all the damage the wind had done to the area. It had blown over the only tree on the entire prairie! It had also lifted some planks from the bridge across the stream but mom did not even think about it. She just jumped over the hole in the bridge and kept on going. When she arrived home, she realized that Spike was not with her. She tried calling for him but, you know, Spike was a fish and could not answer her. So she decided to go looking for him. She backtracked until she got to the bridge and registered the hole in the planking for the first time.

"Oh no, I bet I jumped over that hole without even thinking, and Spike fell in when he tried to do the same thing."

Mom ran to the edge of the hole and looked down. Sure enough, there was old Spike floating in the water—upside down. Spike, the white fish, had drowned!

My mother was furious. She spent all that time training Spike and he goes and drowns on her. She vowed never to have another pet again.

Her parents worried about her attitude and decided that they needed to so something about it. They went to the neighbor and got another small white fish and gave it to mom as a pet. She dumped it into the rain barrel, gave it a name, Spot, and then proceeded to ignore it. Her brothers and sister fed the fish and looked after it as best as they could. One day mom went to check on old Spot and found him swimming around and around in the rain barrel. He had grown so large that the tip of his tail touched his nose.

"This isn't much of a life for a fish," thought my mother. "I am going to set him free."

She put Spot in a pail of water and carried him down to the stream, the same stream in which Spike had drowned. She went to the bank and very gently emptied the pail into the water. She stood there and watched as Spot swam around and around and around.

Spot had never learned to swim straight—all he could do was swim in tight circles! "Oh no, this is all my fault. What will happen if someone wants to catch him?" Just then, out of the corner of her eye, my mom caught sight of an osprey. It was circling the stream, spying out a future meal when suddenly, it began to descend, claws extended, going for Spot. Horrified my mother watched as that osprey started to go around, and around and around, trying to catch Spot. The osprey got dizzy, fell in the water and drowned!

As mom stood there for the next couple of hours, three other ospreys tried to catch Spot, got dizzy, and drowned. After that, mom did not worry about Spot. She worried about the ospreys instead!

Tales of the Arts and Sciences

Three of the four stories in this section have long antecedents: the ancient Indian collection of fables, The Panchatantra; Anglo-Saxon mythology; and a version of the folktale that may have sparked William Shakespeare's *Merchant of Venice*. The fourth tale is an anecdote about the composer Johann Sebastian Bach.

A Pound of Flesh

I briefly discussed this tale in Chapter 8 when speaking of etymologies. A quick search on the Internet results in countless hits of the phrase "a pound of flesh," but rarely, unless it is an academic article, is the origin of the phrase even mentioned. I began telling this tale when I used the term when speaking to young adults and was taken aback, when I realized that they did not know what the phrase meant or from where it sprang. This version is based on "The Young Man and the Lawyer Who Was a Princess." An annotation of a literary adaptation of this tale, "A Gown of Moonthreads," can be also be found in Chapter 8.

There once lived a wealthy Jewish merchant who was blessed with only one son. The merchant loved his son and spoiled him while he was young, thinking that there would be time enough for the boy to mature and become a wise merchant as he himself was. Alas, time did not cooperate, and the rich merchant fell very ill before he had a chance to prepare his son. On his deathbed he asked his son, who was approaching his twentieth year, "What do you plan to do with all that you inherit from me?"

"Ah father, I will do as I have always done. If anyone needs money, I will, of course, give him some. If I meet someone pretty, I will spend money on her, and if I am invited to parties, well, then I will participate with great gusto. What else is money for?"

The father was despondent. "What will become of everything I worked so hard for? What will become of my son?"

Before the father could do anything to protect his finances and his son, he died. And before the year was gone, so was the entire inheritance. The son's friends left as soon as his money disappeared, and he found himself without money, without friends, and without his pride, for he could not stand the shame of being poor. The young man gathered what little he had and traveled to a far-away city, but even there, other rich merchants knew him and his father.

"What are you doing here?" he was asked. "I came on business," was the reply, "but the money has dried up and I find myself without anything at all."

The city may have been far away from the young man's home, but news—good and bad—travels far, and the merchants knew of the young man's spendthrift ways. One merchant, hoping to help the boy learn a lesson, agreed to lend him money. "I will lend you all the money you want, but on one condition.

If you can not repay the loan at the end of the year, you will give me a pound of your flesh."

The young man agreed immediately, thinking that he had an entire year to use this money to make more. He signed a promissory note and went gladly on his way. But alas, the young man did not know how to conduct business successfully, and before the year was out, the money was gone. The loan was due and the young man was terrified for he knew he had to pay the forfeit.

Filled with loathing for his self and pity for his predicament, the young man looked for way out. He could not kill himself, so he came up with another plan. He made his way to the king's palace where entrance was forbidden to all uninvited—under the pain of death. The young man thought that perhaps, if he tried to break into the palace, the guards would end his pain and life for him. But, as with everything else, he was not successful in this plan either! He couldn't get close enough to the entrance of the palace to even be captured and put to death.

He walked aimlessly about for a long while and then finally collapsed in tears under one of the palace windows. His loud sobbing soon disturbed the princess and drew her to the window. It was dark that night with nary a sliver of moonlight to show her what was below the window. "Are you human or a demon?" the princess called softly. "If you are a demon, please leave immediately. If you are human, come closer so that I can see you and so that you can tell me why you are sobbing so desperately."

The young man moved into the light cast by the princess's candle that she held in the window. "I am not a demon, princess, but a poor man who can not even manage to do away with himself." He told her the story of his father, the wasting of his inheritance, and his agreement with the merchant. "The year is coming quickly to an end and I do not have any money to pay back my debt. I know this man, he will demand his pound of flesh, and I do not know what to do."

The princess brought the young man into the palace, fed him and spoke with him through out the night. By morning, the two had fallen in love and the young man was more despondent than ever: not only was his life forfeit, but also he had fallen deeply in love for the very first time. "Don't worry," soothed the princess, "go home to your residence and await my lawyer."

A message came to him at his residence that he should meet with the lawyer at the courtroom for his trial. The young man, dressed in his very best clothing, slowly made his way to the court. When he arrived there, a young lawyer was waiting for him. "The princess has told me everything. Please relax and trust me."

The trial soon began and the merchant told the judge of the agreement. "He can not pay back the money, I am here for the pound of flesh as he agreed, your honor," insisted the rich merchant. The merchant gave the promissory note to the judge.

"Is this your signature?" the judge asked the young man.

"Yes, but I was coerced into signing it!"

"Please answer the question. Is this your signature?"

"Yes, your honor."

"Do you have the money to pay back the loan?"

"No, your honor."

"Do you have anything to say in your defense?"

At this point the lawyer stood up and approached the judge. "Your honor, my client agrees to give the merchant a pound of his flesh as was written in the agreement. I am here to make sure that the pound of flesh is taken in exact measurement. If the merchant takes too little or too much in his first cut, then he must pay the difference with his own flesh."

The merchant, who was very fond of his own flesh, quickly decided that he, not the young man, would forfeit the loan payment and penalty. The case was quickly dismissed. The young man looked for his lawyer, but when he could not be found, retired to his residence again.

He hadn't waited too long when there was a knock on the door. The young man opened the door and the princess entered with a large smile on her face. "Congratulations are in order, I hear. What did you think of the lawyer that I sent?"

"The lawyer was fantastic. He saved my life."

The princess laughed. "Not he, my love. The lawyer was me!"

There was even more laughter and celebration after this announcement. With the princess's help, the young man had learned the lesson the merchant had hoped to teach him, and settled down to regain his father's inheritance. Of course, it did not hurt that his wife was not only a princess, but very clever.

Snake Back Ride

by Merle Harris

Merle says, "This is one of the many stories from the Indian Panchatantra (Five Lessons) my stepfather would tell me. The stories are said to have been written 2000 years ago to teach a kings' sons, not only the scriptures but the wisdom found in them." The stories of the Panchatantra were teaching tools and have been reprinted and repeated since they were first written. The lessons in these tales are as important today as they were when they first were told.

There was once a large pond inhabited in one area by many, many frogs. A large black snake named Slow-Poison lived nearby and feasted daily on unsuspecting frogs.

Water-Foot, the king of the frogs was alarmed at how many frogs were being eaten and advised the frogs to be more alert and to warn the others when they knew Slow-Poison was around.

For a number of days, the snake would slither down to the pond to find no frogs. He had to admit the frogs were clever. However, he was not about to be outsmarted by a bunch of frogs and he went off to find a solution to his problem.

The next morning a frog noticed Slow-Poison draped over a large rock looking thin and its skin tinged with grey.

"Snake," the frog croaked, "are you alright?"

"Sadly, no." hissed the snake. "As you can see I'm fading away. I hadn't been able to catch frogs here for days. Yesterday I went to the far side of the pond to search for food. I spied a plump frog and slithered up to catch it. Standing in the water, close to the frog, were two pious men reciting scripture. As I struck at the frog, one man flung his arm out and I sank my fangs into it and despite my name, he died immediately. His partner put a curse on me. I must now become a carrier of frogs. I cannot chase frogs and can eat only what Water-Foot allows me."

"A carrier of frogs?" queried the frog.

"Yes," hissed the snake, "in order to survive I must carry frogs on my back each day."

The frog was delighted to hear this and rushed off to alert Water-Foot. The king, followed by his queen, children, entourage, servants and common frogs raced off to the snake.

The king asked the snake to repeat his story, and was satisfied when the snake made no attempt to catch any of the frogs. The king climbed on the snake's back, right behind its head, and instructed the other frogs to climb on behind him. As long as the snake was, there was not enough room on his back for all the common frogs so the king instructed them to run alongside or wait.

When they were all ready Slow-Poison called out "Hang on tight for the ride of your life!" and slithered down the rock gathering speed as he went. He went faster and faster, through grass, the shallows of the pond, up and over stones and rocks, twisting and turning, fast, fancy and furious.

Water-Foot, right up in the front was terrified to begin with but soon began to enjoy the speed, the sounds, and the colors. By the time the snake slithered to a stop draped over the rock it had started from, the king was in his element and wanted the ride to continue.

The king was the last to dismount and he called out to the snake as he returned to his home "Same time tomorrow for another snake back ride."

The next morning all the frogs climbed up on the snake's back and the snake called out "Hang on tight for the ride of your life!" but this time he moved very sluggishly, there was no speed, the king could barely feel they were moving.

"Come on Slow-Poison, faster!" called the king, "Give me the fast snake back ride of yesterday."

The snake replied, "Sorry your majesty, I can not go any faster. Have you not forgotten I am not allowed to chase frogs, I have not eaten for days, I have no energy to go any faster."

The king, with no hesitation called out "My dear Slow-Poison, that will never do, eat a couple of the common frogs."

The snake quickly swallowed some frogs and off he went. The ride was even faster and more amazing than the day before. The king enjoyed himself even more than the day before and climbed down with great regret.

That night, the king could think of nothing but the ride he would have the following day and he was down waiting at the rock before the snake arrived. "Eat up, snake," called the king frog, "build up your energy for my snake back ride."

This continued for a number of days, and by now the king lived only for his snake back ride each day, all his other duties were set aside. He daydreamed the speed, the thrill, the joy of the snake back ride.

"Eat up snake!" he called one day but the snake replied, "Your majesty, there are no common frogs left." and he started off slow and sluggish once again. "Wait," called the king "Eat some of the servant frogs." The snake gobbled up a couple of servants and off he went fast and furious.

This continued for more days. By now the king was totally obsessed with his daily snake back ride. He was barely sleeping at night, all he could think of was his daily snake back ride. He was totally unaware of anything else happening.

One day the king leaped up on the snake's back calling "Eat up snake, I must have my snake back ride."

"Your majesty," hissed the snake, "the only frogs left are you and your family."

The king frog hopped down, "Oh dear, what do I do? I love my family more than life itself!"

Then he hopped back on the snake's back, "Eat the youngest quickly, and let's get going."

Soon his children were also gone. "Your majesty," the snake pointed out, "the only frogs remaining are you and your wife."

"What to do, what to do? Only my wife left, you've eaten all the rest?" called out the king, "I cannot go without my snake back ride. Oh snake, eat my wife, but do it quickly!"

At that Slow-Poison quickly swallowed both the king and queen and then slithered off around the pond to find another group of unsuspecting frogs.

A Winter Tale

I developed this tale for a Christmas baroque music concert performed by the Alberta Baroque Society. My telling of the story was recorded and broadcast on CBC radio but has not appeared in print before. The main resource was the Bach Reader: A Life of Johann Sebastian Bach in Letters and Documents *edited by Hans T. David and Arthur Mendel. I include it here as an example of a story that can be told to make the lives and accomplishments of authors, composers, historians, mathematicians, and scientists relevant to those who are now studying them.*

A journey, especially on the frozen paths of winter, is shortened considerably by pleasurable companions. Sometimes this companion is a friend, a colleague, or a family member, but at other times, the companion may be internal—sparkling thoughts or the fever of anticipation. Johann Sebastian Bach was no stranger to journeys. His companions and directions often varied but there was one constant. It was the memory of one journey in particular, a journey that made a lasting impression on him and one that he often spoke of in later years. This journey was undertaken when he was only sixteen, by himself, empty of pocket, and warmed only by the recollection of fine music and spectacular organ playing.

At this time, Sebastian was a student at a school in Luneberg, free to members of the matins choir, which was made up of poor boys with good voices. Sebastian had been welcomed eagerly when he was younger, for he had an usually fine treble voice. His voice had since changed, but he remained an integral part of the choir, a talented instrumentalist. He was constantly curious and innovative in his playing and soon caught the ear of George Bohm, the school's organ teacher. Bohm encouraged Sebastian to seek out Bohm's own teacher, Johann Adam Reincken, in nearby Hamburg for further instruction. Reincken was considered the father of the north German school of music and was well known for his showy playing and the exploitation of all the resources of the organ and there was a particularly fine one in Catharinenkirche where he was the organist.

Sebastian made several trips to Hamburg, walking the fifty kilometers in eager anticipation each time. It was on one of the return journeys that Sebastian had an interesting adventure. Being unable to tear himself away from the heady atmosphere in Hamburg, he left late and without more than a few schillings in his pocket. He was half way home, tired and almost overcome with hunger when he reached an inn.

The savory odors from the kitchen stopped him in his tracks. His thoughts fled from the splendor of the music to something much more mundane: how would he fill the hole in his stomach. While deliberating on what to do, he heard the grinding noise of a window being raised in the inn. Sebastian turned and watched as two herring heads were thrown onto a snow covered rubbish heap. The window then dropped but Sebastian was no longer paying it any mind. He was not only hungry but he was a Thuringian to whom fish was a delicacy!

His mouth began to water. His feet and then his hands made short work of the journey to the rubbish heap and he lost no time in plucking the heads from the snow and picking them clean one at a time. To his surprise the heads contained more than a delectable treat, for inside each head was hidden a Danish ducat.

Totally dumbfounded, Sebastian looked at the ducats and then looked to the window. There was no one there. Sebastian did not waste much time speculating on this turn of events. He immediately went inside the inn and had himself a fine meal to follow his delectable appetizer. The rest of his journey was taken in a daze.

Sebastian never found the identity of his benefactor or any reason for such a generous action. What he did do was undertake another journey, at the first opportunity and in greater comfort, back to Hamburg and Mr. Reincken and his marvelous music.

Twenty years later, Sebastian undertook his final journey to Mr. Reincken in Hamburg. Mr. Reincken was ninety-seven years old at that December meeting. Sebastian, although not seriously considering the position of organist, was auditioning before him. Mr. Reincken was a member of the selection committee and submitted to Sebastian a theme for a fugue treatment as part of the audition. Sebastian played his version of the fugue for his mentor and delighted Reincken with his adaptation. He then took his leave, refusing the offered position. Later, in memory of this occasion, Sebastian wrote out the fugue, the great G Minor Fugue that is still so very popular today.

In the twenty years separating the two winter journeys, Sebastian matured as a musician and composer and in fact reworked several of Reincken's sonatas as his own. His "fishy" benefactor remained unknown, and we can but only speculate if the gift giver ever knew the identity of the recipient of his gift and the longevity of his action.

Woden's Wagon

This is another example of a story that is related to word origins. Woden's Day became our Wednesday, and although this is not a common story about the constellation Ursa Major, it is one that reaches far back to the time when people looked to the stars for inspirations and explanations.

The belief in Woden's Hunt lived long and vividly in native story and folklore: it still continues to do so in the superstition (suitably revamped by Christians) of Gabriel's Hounds; while as recently as 1939 the myth has reappeared in a popular American cowboy song, the "Riders in the Sky," in which the homeless dead are a ghostly "devil's herd" of cattle whose "brands wuz still on fire" and whose "hooves wuz made of steel," while Woden is represented as a ghostly cowboy condemned to a terrible eternity of rounding-up "across these endless skies." (Branston, 94)

The seven brightest stars of the constellation known as Ursa Major (the Great Bear) form the shape of what is commonly known as the Big Dipper. But this shape also forms the constellation that has been known for thousands of years as Woden's Wagon.

Woden was the chief and father of the gods. With his brothers, he fashioned the earth and the sky from the dead body of the giant Ymir, and from an ash tree and an alder, he created the first man and woman. Although widely known as a god of war, he was important as a god of learning, of poetry, and, above all, of magic. He was a shape changer, able to take on any form, but it is said that he liked to travel best disguised as an old man with a staff—one-eyed, grey-bearded, and wearing a wide-brimmed hat.

He was a compulsive seeker of wisdom, so much so that he sacrificed one eye, was hanged on the tree Yggdrasil for nine days and nine nights, and was voluntarily pierced with a spear in effort to gain more wisdom and the secret of the runes. (The creation of the runes, the Norse alphabet that was also used for divination, is attributed to Woden (Odin) and is described in the Havamal, part of the *Poetic Edda*.) The magical artifacts associated with him include the dwarven spear "Gungrni"; a magical gold ring; an eight-legged horse "Sleipnir"; two wolves, Geri and Freki; and the two ravens, Hugin (Thought) and Munin (Memory), who travel the world to gather information for him when not riding on his shoulders. All of these artifacts have stories attached to them, but none is so visible as his wagon in the night sky.

173

As you stand out in the night watching Woden's Wagon make its rounds, do not be surprised if you hear a howling wind, the type of wind that sends shivers down your back, the type of wind that makes you long for safety and shelter. And be aware that this wind is more than an ordinary wind; it is the sound of Woden's Wagon on the move. And if the night is clear you may see the bright star in the constellation, directly above the centre star of the wagon shaft, called the driver. The driver rides an eight-legged horse that is pulling the wagon. This driver, so the story tells, was promised the kingdom of heaven. He laughed and replied, "I would rather drive for eternity from the rising to the setting of the stars just as the wild hunter would rather hunt for eternity." The driver got his wish and can be seen guiding Woden's Wagon across the northern sky. And the hunt, the wild hunt attributed to Woden, among others, can be heard at every turn of the wheels.

References

Branston, Brian. 1974. *The Lost Gods of England.* New York: Oxford University Press.

Crowley, Catherine. 1999. The Phantom Ahead. *Storytelling World* 16(summer/fall): 8.

David, Hans T., and Arthur Mendel. *Bach Reader: A Life of Johann Sebastian Bach in Letters and Documents.* New York: W. W. Norton, 1945.

Jaffe, Nina, and Steve Zeitlin, 1998. *The Cow of No Color: Riddle Stories and Justice Tales from Around the World.* New York: Henry Holt.

Sadeh, Pinhas. 1989. The Young Man and the Lawyer Who Was a Princess. In *Jewish Folktales.* New York: Doubleday, 277–79.

Snyder, Midori. 1987. The First Soulstring. *Soulstring.* New York: Ace, 101–103.

Spagnoli, Cathy. 1999. King's Questions. In *Jasmine and Coconuts: South Indian Tales,* by Cathy Spagnoli and Paramasivam Samanna. Englewood, CO: Libraries Unlimited, 94.

Stotter, Ruth. The Twelve Months. In *The Golden Axe and Other Folk Tales of Compassion and Greed.* Oakland, CA: Stotter Press, pp. 20–22.

Yashinsky, Dan. 1997. *Ghostwise: A Book of Midnight Stories.* Charlottetown, PEI: Ragweed Press, 87–90.

Yashinsky, Dan, collector. 1994. *Next Teller: A Book of Canadian Storytelling.* Charlottetown, PEI: Ragweed Press, 15–19

Yashinsky, Dan. (forthcoming). Why All Tongues Are Red. In *Suddenly They Heard Footsteps.* Toronto: Alfred A. Knopf Canada.

Author Index

Title Index

Note: Stories presented in full in this book are in a bold typeface.

Theme Index

Note: Stories that are presented in full in this book are in a bold typeface.

Story Collections

*Asterisk denotes single-story volumes
**Two asterisks denotes a novel rather than a collection of stories

Andrews, Jan, reteller. 2000. *Out of the Everywhere: Tales for a New World.* Toronto: Groundwood.

Baltuck, Naomi, reteller. 1995. *Apples from Heaven: Multicultural Folk Tales about Stories and Storytellers.* North Haven, CT: Linnet.

Batt, Tanya Robyn, reteller. 2000. *The Fabrics of Fairytale: Stories Spun from Far and Wide.* New York: Barefoot.

**Block, Francesca Lia. 2001. *echo.* New York: Joanna Cotler.

Bruchac, Joseph, reteller. 1995. *Native Plant Stories.* Golden, CO: Fulcrum.

Bruchac, Joseph, and James Bruchac. 1998. *When the Chenoo Howls: Native American Tales of Terror.* New York: Walker.

Bruchac, Joseph, and Gayle Ross, retellers. 1994. *The Girl Who Married the Moon: Tales from Native North America.* New York: Bridgewater.

*Carlson, Laurie. 1998. *Boss of the Plains: The Hat That Won the West.* Illustrations by Holly Meade. New York.

Carter, Angela, editor. 1992. *The Second Virago Book of Fairy Tales.* London: Virago Press.

Carter, Angela, editor. 1990. *The Old Wives' Fairy Tale Book.* New York: The Pantheon Fairy Tale and Folklore Library.

Congdon, Kristin G. 2001. *Uncle Monday and Other Florida Tales.* Illustrated by Kitty Kitson Petterson. Jackson: University of Mississippi.

Curry, Lindy Soon, reteller. 1999. *A Tiger by the Tail and Other Stories from the Heart of Korea.* Englewood, CO: Libraries Unlimited.

Czarnota, Lorna MacDonald. 2000. *Medieval Tales That Kids Can Read and Tell.* Little Rock, AR: August House.

DeSpain, Pleasant. 1999. *The Emerald Lizard: Fifteen Latin American Tales to Tell in English and Spanish.* Little Rock, AR: August House

203

DeSpain, Pleasant. 2000. *Sweet Land of Story: Thirty-Six American Tales to Tell*. Little Rock, AR: August House

DeSpain, Pleasant, reteller. 2001. *Tales of Tricksters* (The Books of Nine Lives, Vol. 1) Little Rock, AR: August House.

DeSpain, Pleasant, reteller. 2001. *Tales of Wisdom & Justice* (The Books of Nine Lives, Vol. 3) Little Rock, AR: August House.

Doherty, Berlie. 1997. *Tales of Wonder and Magic*. Cambridge, MA: Candlewick.

Doyle, Malachy, reteller. 2000. *Tales from Old Ireland*. New York: Barefoot Books.

Eisner, Will. 2000. *Minor Miracles*. New York: DC Comics.

Evetts-Secker, Josephine, reteller. 1997. *Father and Daughter Tales*. London: Barefoot Books.

Evetts-Secker, Josephine, reteller. 1996. *Mother and Daughter Tales*. London: Barefoot Books.

Forest, Heather, reteller. 1995. *Wonder Tales from Around the World*. Little Rock, AR: August House.

Fradin, Dennis Brindell. 2000. *Bound for the North Star: True Stories of Fugitive Slaves*. New York: Clarion.

French, Vivian. 1997. In *Breaking the Spell: Tales of Enchantment*. Selected by Sally Grindley. New York: Kingfisher.

Gignoux, Jane Hughes. 1998. *Some Folk Say: Stories of Life, Death, and Beyond*. New York: FoulkeTale Publishing.

Gilchrist, Cherry, reteller. 1998. *A Calendar of Festivals*. Bristol, UK: Barefoot

Hamilton, Martha, and Mitch Weiss, 2000. *Noodlehead Stories: World Tales Kids Can Read & Tell*. Little Rock, AR: August House.

Hamilton, Martha, and Mitch Weiss, retellers. 2001. *Through the Grapevine: World Tales Kids Can Read & Tell*. Little Rock, AR: August House.

Hamilton, Virginia. 1995. *Her Stories: African American Folktales, Fairy Tales and True Tales*. New York: Blue Sky.

Hamilton, Virginia. 1997. *A Ring of Tricksters: Animal Tales from America, the West Indies and Africa*. New York: Blue Sky Press.

Hausman, Gerald, and Hausman, Loretta. 2000. *Cats of Myth: Tales from Around the World*. New York: Simon & Schuster.

Hoffman, Mary, and Jane Ray. 1998. *Sun, Moon and Stars*. London: Orion.

Holt, David, and Bill Mooney, editors. 1994. In *Ready-to-Tell Tales: Sure-Fire Stories from America's Favorite Storytellers*. Little Rock, AR: August House.

Husain, Shahrukh. 1995. *Handsome Heroines: Women as Men in Folklore*, New York: Anchor.

Husain, Shahrukh, reteller. 1999. *Stories from the Opera.* New York: Barefoot Books.

Husain, Shahrukh, editor. 1993. *The Virago Book of Witches.* London: Virago.

Jaffe, Nina, and Steve Zeitlin, retellers. 1998. *The Cow of No Color: Riddle Stories and Justice Tales from Around the World.* New York: Henry Holt.

Kane, Alice, reteller. 1995. *The Dreamer Awakes.* Peterborough, ON: Broadview Press.

Krull, Kathleen. 1995. *Lives of the Artists: Masterpieces, Messes (and What the Neighbors Thought).* San Diego, CA: Harcourt Brace.

Krull, Kathleen. 1997. *Lives of the Athletes: Thrills, Spills (and What the Neighbors Thought).* San Diego, CA: Harcourt Brace.

Krull, Kathleen. 1993. *Lives of the Musicians: Good Times, Bad Times (and What the Neighbors Thought).* San Diego, CA: Harcourt Brace.

Krull, Kathleen. 1994. *Lives of the Writers: Comedies, Tragedies (and What the Neighbors Thought).* San Diego, CA: Harcourt Brace.

Krull, Kathleen. 1999. *They Saw the Future: Oracles, Psychics, Scientists, Great Thinkers, and Pretty Good Guessers.* New York: Atheneum.

Leeming, David, and Jake Page. 1999. *Myths, Legends, and Folktales of America: An Anthology.* Oxford: Oxford University Press.

Lewis, I. Murphy, collector. 1997. *Why Ostriches Don't Fly and Other Tales from the African Bush.* Englewood, CO: Libraries Unlimited.

*Littlesugar, Amy. 1998. *Shake Rag: From the Life of Elvis Presley.* Illustrated by Floyd Cooper. New York: Philomel.

Livo, Norma J. 2001. *Story Medicine: Multicultural Tales of Healing and Transformation.* Englewood, CO: Libraries Unlimited.

Livo, Norma J., and Dia Cha. (1991) *Folk Stories of the Hmong: Peoples of Laos, Thailand, and Vietnam.* Englewood, CO: Libraries Unlimited.

*Lottridge, Celia Barker. 1998. *Music for the Tsar of the Sea.* Illustrations by Harvey Chan. Toronto: Groundwood

Louis, Liliane Nerette. 1999. *When Night Falls, Kric! Krac! Haitian Folktales.* (World Folklore Series). Englewood, CO: Libraries Unlimited.

MacDonald, Margaret Read, reteller. 1999. *Earth Care: World Folktales to Talk About.* North Haven, CT: Linnet.

MacDonald, Margaret Read, reteller. 1995. *Ghost Stories from the Pacific Northwest*, Little Rock, AR: August House.

Mama, Raouf, translator and reteller. 1998. *Why Goats Smell Bad and Other Stories from Benin.* North Haven, CT: Linnet.

**Marillier, Juliet. 2001. *Son of Shadows.* New York: TOR.

Marshall, Bonnie C., reteller. 2001. *Tales from the Heart of the Balkans.* Englewood, CO: Libraries Unlimited.

Martin, Rafe, reteller. 1996. *Mysterious Tales of Japan.* New York: G.P. Putnam's Sons.

Matthews, John, reteller. 1999. *Giants, Ghosts and Goblins: Traditional Tales from Around the World.* New York: Barefoot Books.

Matthews, John, and Matthews, Caitlin. 1998. *The Wizard King & Other Spellbinding Tales.* New York: Barefoot Books

Max, Jill. Ed. 1997. *Spider Spins a Story: Fourteen Legends from Native America.* Flagstaff, AZ: Northland.

Mayo, Margaret, reteller. 1996. *Mythical Birds and Beasts from Many Lands.* New York: Dutton.

Mayo, Margaret, reteller. 1995. *When the World Was Young: Creation and Pourquoi Tales.* New York: Simon & Schuster.

McBride-Smith, Barbara. 1998. *Greek Myths, Western Style: Toga Tales with an Attitude.* Little Rock, AR: August House.

McCaughrean, Geraldine, reteller. 1997. *The Bronze Cauldron: Myths and Legends of the World.* London: Orion.

McKay, Helen F. 2001. *Gadi Mirrabooka: Australian Aboriginal Tales from the Dreaming.* Englewood, CO: Libraries Unlimited.

McNeil, Heather. 2001. *The Celtic Breeze: Stories of the Otherworld from Scotland, Ireland and Wales.* Englewood, CO: Libraries Unlimited.

Mendoza, Patrick M., Ann Strange Owl-Raben, and Nico Strange Owl. 1998. *Four Great Rivers to Cross: Cheyenne History, Culture and Traditions.* Englewood, CO: Teachers' Idea Press.

Olson, Arielle North, and Howard Schwartz, retellers. 1999. *Ask the Bones: Scary Stories from Around the World.* New York: Viking.

Osborne, Mary Pope, reteller. 1998. *Favorite Medieval Tales.* New York: Scholastic.

Parent, Michael, and Julien Oliver, retellers. 1996. *Of Kings and Fools: Stories of the French Tradition in North America.* Little Rock, AR: August House.

Philip, Neil, editor. 1999. *Stockings of Buttermilk: American Folktales.* New York: Clarion.

Ragan, Kathleen, editor. 1998. *Fearless Girls, Wise Women, and Beloved Sisters: Heroines in Folktales from Around the World.* New York: W. W. Norton.

Roe, Betty, Suellen Alfred, and Sandy Smith. (1998). *Teaching through Stories: Yours, Mine and Theirs.* Norwood, MA: Christopher-Gordon.

Ross, Gayle, reteller. 1994. *How Rabbit Tricked Otter and Other Cherokee Trickster Stories.* New York: HarperCollins.

*Ross, Gayle, reteller. 1996. *The Legend of the Windigo: A Tale from Native North America.* Illustrations by Murv Jacob. New York: Dial.

San Souci, Robert D. 1993. *Cut from the Same Cloth: American Women of Myth, Legend and Tall Tale.* New York: Philomel.

San Souci, Robert D., reteller. 1998. *A Terrifying Taste of Short & Shivery: Thirty Creepy Tales.* New York: Delacorte.

San Souci, Robert D., reteller. 1997. *Even More Short & Shivery: Thirty Spine-Tingling Tales.* New York: Delacorte.

Schmidt, Gary D. 2001. *Straw into Gold.* New York: Clarion.

*Shepard, Aaron, reteller. 1998. *The Crystal Heart: A Vietnamese Legend.* Illustrated by Joseph Daniel Fiedler. New York: Atheneum.

Sherman, Josepha 1994. *Once Upon a Galaxy: The Ancient Stories Behind Star Wars, Superman and Other Popular Fantasies.* Little Rock, AR: August House.

Sherman, Josepha. 1995. *Told Tales: Nine Folktales from Around the World.* New York: Silver Moon.

Sherman, Josepha, reteller. 1996. *Trickster Tales: Forty Folk Stories from Around the World.* Little Rock, AR: August House.

Shrestha, Kavita Ram, and Sarah Lamstein. 1997. *From the Mango Tree and Other Folktales from Nepal.* Englewood, CO: Libraries Unlimited.

Spagnolli, Cathy, reteller. 1998. *Asian Tales and Tellers.* Little Rock, AR: August House.

Spagnoli, Cathy. 2001. *Terrific Trickster Tales from Asia.* Fort Atkinson, WI: Alleyside Press.

Spagnoli, Cathy, and Paramasivam Samanna. 1999. *Jasmine and Coconuts: South Indian Tales.* Englewood, CO: Libraries Unlimited.

Spariosu, Milhai I., and Dezso Benedek, retellers. 1994. *Ghosts, Vampires, and Werewolves: Eerie Tales from Transylvania.* New York: Orchard Books.

Spencer, Ann. 2001. *Song of the Sea: Myths, Tales and Folklore.* Toronto: Tundra.

Springer, Nancy. 2000. *Ribbiting Tales: Original Stories about Frogs.* New York: Philomel.

Tahan, Malba. 1993. *The Man Who Counted: A Collection of Mathematical Adventures.* Translated by Leslie Clark and Alastair Reid. New York: W. W. Norton.

Tarnowska, Wafa, reteller. 2000. *The Seven Wise Princesses: A Medieval Epic.* New York: Barefoot Books.

Tchana, Katrin. 2000. *The Serpent Slayer and Other Stories of Strong Women*. Boston: Little, Brown and Company.

Terada, Alice. M. 1994. *The Magic Crocodile and Other Folktales from Indonesia*. Honolulu: University of Hawaii Press.

Torrence, Jackie. 1998. *Jackie Tales: The Magic of Creating Stories and the Art of Telling Them*. New York: Avon.

Van Deusen, Kira. 1996. *Shyaan Am! Tuvan Folk Tales*. Bellingham, WA: Udagan Books.

**Wagamese, Richard. 1994. *Keeper'n Me*. Toronto: Doubleday Canada.

Walker, Richard, reteller. 1998. *The Barefoot Book of Pirates*. New York: Barefoot Books.

*Wisniewski, David. 1996. *Golem*. New York: Clarion.

Yashinsky, Dan, collector. 1997. In *ghostwise: A Book of Midnight Stories*. Charlottetown, PEI: Ragweed.

Yashinsky, Dan, collector. 1994. In *Next Teller: A Book of Canadian Storytelling*. Charlottetown, PEI: Ragweed.

Yep, Laurence. 1995. *Tree of Dreams: Ten Tales from the Garden of Night*. New York: Bridgewater.

Yolen, Jane. 1993. *Here There Be Dragons*. San Diego, CA: Harcourt Brace.

Yolen, Jane. 1998. *Here There Be Ghosts*. San Diego, CA: Harcourt Brace.

Yolen, Jane. 1994. *Here There Be Witches*. San Diego, CA: Harcourt Brace.

Yolen, Jane, reteller. 2000. *Not One Damsel in Distress: World Folktales for Strong Girls*. San Diego, CA: Harcourt.

Yolen, Jane. 2000. *Sister Emily's Lightship and Other Stories*. New York: TOR.

Young, Richard, and Judy Dockrey Young. 1993. *The Scary Story Reader: Forty-one of the Scariest Stories for Sleepovers, Campfires, Car & Bus Trips—Even for First Dates*. Little Rock, AR: August House.

Zeitlin, Steve. 2000. *The Four Corners of the Sky: Creation Stories and Cosmologies from Around the World*. New York: Henry Holt.

DATE DUE